With God
All Things are Possible

Maureen Wise

Evangelical Movement of Wales
The EMW works in both Welsh and English and seeks to help Christians and churches by:
- running children's camps and family conferences
- providing theological training and events for ministers
- running Christian bookshops and a conference centre
- publishing magazines and books

Bryntirion Press is a ministry of EMW

Past issues of EMW magazines and sermons preached at our conferences are available on our web site: www.emw.org.uk

Published by Bryntirion Press, Bryntirion, Bridgend CF31 4DX, Wales, in association with EP BOOKS, Faverdale North, Darlington, DL3 0PH, UK.

EP BOOKS are distributed in the USA by:
JPL Fulfillment, 3741 Linden Avenue Southeast, Grand Rapids, MI 49548.
E-mail: sales@jplfulfillment.com
Tel: 877.683.6935

"Having had the privilege to spend some time with the folks mentioned here, I would invite you to take a journey. This book will change you. Why? Because, and I quote Maureen, 'we understood an awareness of a great spiritual battle, and a constant need to be vigilant and to use the full armour of God, and to pray without ceasing'. This battle still rages but Jesus is building his church, and the gates of hell will not prevail against it. Miracles do happen, and when they do 'Bucure a Venit'—joy has arrived!"

Mrs Deborah Woolley, UFM Worldwide Board member and pastor's wife, Cardiff.

"In the West, Christians sometimes equate the kingdom of God with big crowds and big money. This book reminds us that God works powerfully in poverty, darkness, and loneliness—to the praise of His glorious grace. Both those interested in the progress of the gospel in Eastern Europe and those who simply desire to grow in their faith will find inspiration from these accounts by Maureen Wise."

Dr. Joel R. Beeke, President, Puritan Reformed Theological Seminary, Grand Rapids, Michigan

"This account of God moving by His Spirit in Romania and Moldova makes humbling and thrilling reading. Having had the privilege of visiting the latter country, I warmly commend this work, and may it create a desire in our own hearts for the Lord to visit us again in power here in Wales."

Rev. Wyn Hughes, Pastor, Heath Evangelical Church, Cardiff

Contents

Preface

The pages that follow will quickly reveal the struggles of a failing missionary who felt as though she never quite made the grade. It contains the story of a fatally flawed sinner who was brought to the Saviour by His power and mercy alone. That I should be allowed to observe first hand some of His most wonderful works in Romania and Moldova is evidence to me of His most amazing grace and goodness to those who deserve nothing but judgement. There is no grace like His and no forgiveness like His. My hope is that the reader will see beyond those not very brave attempts to adapt to another culture and language to a God who still continues to use earthen vessels "that the excellency of the power may be of God and not of us."

The original purpose of writing was to record what we had seen God do before the detail was lost to our memories. It was intended as a record that might be made accessible to a small group of brothers and sisters in Christ who had prayed for our work from the beginning. The end product may reach a slightly larger readership than that for which it was initially intended. But whatever the readership becomes, my hope would be that it would bring glory only to the Lord Jesus Christ who began and sustains the work of which these pages speak.

I am very indebted to Rev. Owen Milton for the hours without number he has spent poring over and editing the text and for wise advice on the content. His interest in the work is a very real one, enhanced by visits he and his wife have made to Moldova and the work there. Linda Baynham has used her expertise to proof read the text and I am most grateful indeed to her also.

The real heroes of this story are those countless brothers and sisters in Christ in Romania and Moldova whom it has been my great blessing to know and to learn from. So many of them have been as the fragrance of Christ to me. Through them I have seen "the work of faith with power" over and over again. I have learnt from them to have a prayerful dependence on a God who has not the slightest difficulty in doing the impossible. Let us continue to expect great things from Him and to attempt great things for Him and may a younger generation be stirred up to go after this same God for even greater things than we have seen.

1

Early Impressions

*And you shall remember that
the Lord your God led you all the way ...
(Isaiah 43:1)*

The initial buzz of conversation in the plane had quietened as passengers lapsed into reverie or sleep. I was returning from Moldova and, starved of news for the preceding months, I was devouring the contents of a Romanian newspaper I had been given when boarding. My eyes fell on a cartoon. It was December 2006 and Romania was about to join the European Union. The cartoon depicted the President of Romania, European flag in hand, triumphantly looking westwards and running with all speed towards Europe. The Republic of Moldova, although in reality geographically sharing a border with Romania, was, in the cartoon, separated from Romania. Its Communist President, Voronin, was looking wistfully eastwards towards Russia. Tears dropped from the map of Moldova—tears of grief for its desperate plight—and under the Republic of Transnistria (a part of Moldova occupied by Russia's powerful 14th Army), there were tears of blood. The tears of blood commemorated those who had died in the civil war occasioned by Russia's occupation of part of Moldova's territory in 1991. There was no inscription for the cartoon. None was needed. The picture was a powerful one and captured vividly Moldova's suffering and political isolation. Part of me identified strongly with the plight of this country to which God had called me and whose people I had come to love.

There was no doubt that the political and economic realities for Moldova at the time were harsh. It was the poorest country in Europe and was still reeling from the collapse of its economy following the demise of the Soviet Union, of which it had been a part. During the 1990s particularly, unemployment was colossally high as Moldova had lost its main export markets. Many older people had lost all their savings overnight when the currency changed from roubles to Moldovan lei. It was believed that the only ones who had escaped this huge economic disaster were those politicians who had prior knowledge of the change and had transferred their money in time. My first visit to Moldova took place in the nineties. As I walked around the city of Chișinău I remember being struck by the sight of people lining the central streets with some of their meagre possessions displayed on the ground in front of them in the vain hope that someone would make a purchase. Sometimes,

I noticed, they would stand there all day in bitter weather. The city looked like a desolate industrial wasteland in those days. It was clearly in a ruinous state, with factories deserted and derelict. My new Moldovan friends recounted stories of local people being attacked in the streets and their money stolen. Sometimes they were killed. Apartments were frequently broken into. The electricity went off at regular intervals. Alcoholism was clearly a significant problem. There was an indescribable bleakness everywhere.

The Moldovan winter is hard and relentless and pleasant visions of glistening snow and sledges soon disappear in the midst of some of the grimmer realities of day to day life. Leisure and free time, it seems to me, are purely Western inventions and I had learnt from living previously in Romania that life for Christians there was generally about very hard work and any free time was devoted to service in the church and worship. Life is a little easier these days in Romania for many, but then much time was also taken up by household activities without the helps that we in the West normally take for granted. Shopping in the market and then carrying heavy bags full of food home on a crowded tram would take hours. Queuing for a very long time to try to buy milk, and then realising the milk supply had finished just as the head of the queue was reached, was a common experience. Paying bills frequently resulted in public humiliation if you made any attempt to argue that the bill you had received was larger than it should have been.

Sometimes when I was in Romania people would send me parcels. What an adventure that always proved to be! A visit by tram to the nearest large post office where parcels were kept was inevitably followed by a wait in a very long queue.

When the head of the queue was reached, the official behind a desk, having eventually found the parcel in question, would proceed to tear the package apart in full view of a large crowd of interested onlookers. However precious the contents might be, receiving parcels in such a fashion quickly lost its attraction.

Life in Moldova was in many ways similar to those earlier days in Romania, but the context was harsher and life for most people was tougher. Summer months were much easier—days full of sunshine and warmth and fields crowded with huge sunflowers constantly turning their heads in the direction of the light. Fruit and vegetables would be in plentiful supply and there were apricot, cherry and walnut trees everywhere. People worked very hard on the land during those brief summer months. Groups of workers would be seen, bent over the swiftly growing plants in the blazing sun, heads covered with scarves or handkerchiefs and faces reddened by prolonged exposure to the elements. Brief periods of respite would see them sitting on the ground in a group, drinking from large containers and eating great hunks of bread.

The vineyards would somehow recover quickly, even from the hardest of winters, as soon as the summer began in earnest and their shiny green foliage would fill the countryside. Horses or donkeys could be seen pulling carts full of produce and passengers and usually struggling under the weight of their load. Villagers would paint their houses and their fences again, and bright blues and yellows and greens would greet you as you drove by. Golden, onion-shaped cupolas on Orthodox churches would shine in the reflected sunlight and marked the landscape from afar.

Geese would claim right of way in every track and would only with great reluctance and noisy protest move aside. Goats, even when tethered, would nonchalantly munch through everything in their immediate vicinity. The village wells, usually elaborately decorated with religious symbols and ornate silver trellises, became busy talking-points for villagers as they drew water and filled pails and plastic containers.

Winter was another story. Those who have lived in such countries will know that there is a desperate drabness to those long winter months. By the end of winter I always had a strong feeling of sensory deprivation. There was very little of beauty to look at, particularly in the numerous large housing estates. Tall, poorly constructed and already decaying blocks of flats were typical dwelling places for most people in the city. Cold, dark and usually dirty entrances to such blocks led to a lift that broke down very often and, even when working, creaked its way up with alarming clatter.

Although in later years those who were well off could buy virtually anything in Chişinău, those with whom I lived would rarely buy fresh fruit or vegetables in the winter because they were too expensive. That would be fairly usual for the great majority of families in the capital. Home comforts were in short supply, but one soon became accustomed to this.

The cold weather arrived early and it was not uncommon for it to snow at the beginning of November. Those living in blocks of flats would be subject to the vagaries of the central heating system controlled by the city council, and the heating would not usually be turned on until mid- or even late November. By this time the whole city would be shivering. Most people coped with the rigours of the cold stoically, but I always found this one of the more difficult features of life. To return to a bitterly cold flat from harsh winds and snow outside was far from easy. Sometimes, while preparing for teaching, I would be wrapped in a blanket in an attempt to keep warm. With what pleasure and thankfulness we greeted the day when the heating would finally be switched on!

Working life always started very early in the morning and quite often we would all be out of the house by 6.30 facing icy cold and almost total darkness. Packs of stray dogs would be roaming around always looking desperately hungry, yet afraid if anyone approached them. A fair distance of walking across frozen and uneven paths at last brought us to the trolleybus stop. Crowds of people, often wearing Soviet-style fur hats and their heaviest outdoor garb, would be gathered in the semi-darkness. Their breath could be seen against the very dim lights from the road. The arrival of the trolleybus saw a full-scale disorderly rush as people tried to cram onto the steps of the vehicle and squeeze into every available space before the doors rattled shut. The conductor had the most unenviable task of somehow pushing his or her way through the closely packed mass of passengers in an often vain attempt to extract fares from those unwilling to pay. Vociferous arguments would erupt if any refused to pay. And so the transport heaved and swayed its tortuous way into town.

These were some of the practical privations. None of them was particularly gruelling and with time they became an ordinary and accepted part of my everyday life. But added to them were the challenges of living in a country where, to all appearances, bureaucracy and corruption reigned almost unrestrained. With very few exceptions officials were rude and obstructive, and there were interminable battles to be fought if you were in search of any official permission to take a certain step. The only course was to take a deep breath, pray much, and then run the gauntlet of a host of officious individuals seemingly taking great delight in doing all within their power to obstruct your cause. These encounters could take hours and days and the end result would quite often be failure on your part to achieve your goal.

Together with this, along with the consciousness of the Lord being powerfully at work, there was the awareness of being in the most ferocious spiritual battle. It was as if the great enemy of souls was more frequently unmasked in Moldova than I had previously known, and there was a constant need to be vigilant and to use the full armour of God and to try to pray without ceasing. One winter it felt as though we were confronting assault after assault in the spiritual realm, and at every step it was necessary to arm ourselves with the Word and with prayer. The Scriptures which told us that "For this purpose the Son of God was manifested, that he might destroy the works of the devil" (1 John 3:8) and that the Lord has "delivered us from the power of darkness" (Colossians 1:13) were assurances to which we resorted frequently.

One night, unable to sleep, I wondered if I really would be able to cope with the rigours, spiritual and practical, of another such winter and if the Lord really would renew my strength. As I did, a verse of Scripture came powerfully into my consciousness. "Neither will I offer ... unto the Lord my

God of that which doth cost me nothing" (2 Samuel 24:24 (AV))." And there was my answer. Why should I be in the least surprised if my Saviour, in his excellent and loving purposes, should ask of me service which I found personally costly? He was the One who had experienced the pains of Golgotha for me, and had told me that my life was not my own, that I was bought with a price.

I had been meditating in the previous months on the words of Jesus in the Gospel according to Mark: "For whoever desires to save his life will lose it, but whoever loses his life for My sake and the gospel's will save it" (Mark 8:35). I reflected that this was what it meant to take up the cross daily to follow Him. It involved a determination to go after Him at all costs, a cost which certainly took little account of our fleshly instincts or natural desires. Being in step with Him often meant being out of step with our friends with their plans and preoccupations, enduring hardness as a good soldier of Jesus Christ. This was what it was to love a Redeemer who had sacrificed Himself for me.

I once heard an illustration I have never forgotten. It was about a tree that would be needed as a beam in an ancient cathedral to support the roof, and the quality of the wood required for that purpose. A young sapling would be planted with a small group of other young trees just above the tree line on a mountain. Over a long period of time the other trees would be removed one by one until it alone was left to face the elements. It would be exposed to the relentless winds and storms and blizzards of winter. The effect would be either to weaken the tree or to strengthen it for use in the cathedral. The point of the illustration is perhaps obvious: God will sometimes so work in our lives that we are left without human support in order that we may lean only upon Him, and so be prepared for the work He has in store for us.

At the back of my Bible I have written a quotation from A. W. Tozer: "God will not use a man greatly until he has broken him deeply." In my case I feel that He has allowed me to see something of His powerful hand at work, albeit most often as an almost passive observer. The Lord Himself is the author and very careful engineer of brokenness in our lives. It will not come in the same way for all His children, but it will always be skilfully supervised by Him for His glorious and sometimes secret purposes. Someone who can say from his heart "Like a weaned child is my soul within me" (Psalm 131:2) will know the peace which accompanies a trustful submission.

2

Conversion and Call

God is able to raise up children
to Abraham from these stones
(Matthew 3:9; Luke 3:8)

The path that led me to Moldova began, as do many spiritual journeys, at school. I was converted at the age of seventeen. Looking back I am not aware of any truly Christian influence at all in my childhood. My father had had a career in the army and in those days was opposed to Christian things, as far as I remember. I had no contact with church, apart from an occasional wedding, or with Sunday school. With regard to the Gospel, I was totally ignorant. Brought up on a council housing estate in London, I seem to recall that there was only one family in our whole street that attended church regularly and that was a Roman

Catholic family. My mother was herself a lapsed Roman Catholic who hailed from Southern Ireland. She had strong sympathies with the Sinn Fein cause and I grew up learning some of the Republican protest songs and ballads.

At the age of about eight, I have a strong recollection of saying to myself one night that there was no God, so I could do as I pleased. I was sent to a young person's club regularly. My father had very left-wing political leanings and it was only in retrospect that I realised that the club to which he sent me was communist in its affiliation. Each summer an under-canvas camp would be arranged by the club and I happily attended. One summer I can remember that for some reason a young friend and I were talking about God and church—we could not have been more than about ten years old at the time. I can distinctly remember that the camp leader, to whom I looked up with great respect and warmth, mocked our discussion and told us that there was no God. Despite my earlier affirmation to myself that there was no God, I was both horrified and confused to hear this from an adult of whom I thought highly.

School days passed happily enough. I enjoyed things academic and managed to do well. By the time I arrived in the sixth form, however, an earnest spiritual quest arose in my consciousness. A day arrived which I remember very clearly, when during a lesson my attention strayed and I was gazing out of the classroom window. Despite being in inner London, the view which greeted me held me spellbound. It was as if I was looking at a row of splendid poplar trees and a radiant blue sky for the first time and realised that there must have been a God who had created such beauty. This awareness gripped my heart and I knew that I had to begin to try to find this God.

But where to begin? I can remember asking Him to reveal Himself to me. Sometime previously each of us at school had been presented with a Bible on behalf of the school. I had barely opened it, but sought for it at home and began to read it. Without the slightest understanding of spiritual things I began to seek with all my heart for the One of whom I had had a glimpse through His creation. My soul was hungry and thirsty for Him and I reckoned with myself that perhaps I would find Him in this book. With what attention I devoured the words I was reading in the Scriptures!

With no background at all in Christian truths, it is difficult to describe the degree of darkness in which my soul was found. "Fast bound in sin and nature's night" was an accurate description of my state. But as I read the Scriptures they began to speak to me with great conviction. I understood without any doubt that this Lord Jesus Christ was the Son of God and that He was the only way to heaven. Although my spiritual understanding was very limited indeed, I knew that I had found the One who was to be the centre and the goal of my whole life—this Saviour who alone could truly satisfy my soul. I read in the Word that "if anyone is in Christ, he is a new creation; old things have passed away; behold all things have become new" (2 Corinthians 5:17). It was obvious to me that I had been born again and that my life had changed beyond recognition. In terms of my grasp of the Word, it was weak, but despite that His hold on me was strong.

I felt just as though I had been sitting in a cellar of total spiritual darkness which was suddenly flooded with light.

Although my spiritual sight was still like that of the blind man whose eyes Jesus had opened and who saw men indistinctly, it was enough. The Lord Himself had intervened in my sinful, lost life and had taken me from the power of darkness and put me into the kingdom of His Son. Here was a God who, by His own power, had snatched me from the road to hell. It was He that had first planted in my soul a longing after Himself. Here was a God who was able to do the truly impossible and whose Son was able to save completely all who trust in Him.

Having become quite sure that I was converted, and beginning to tell my friends and family that I had become a Christian, a realisation began to dawn on me that I should be attending a church. But which church should I go to? I had not the slightest idea. In the absence of any sense about which church I should choose, I decided simply to go to the one that was nearest. In God's great kindness this turned out to be an evangelical Anglican church. Here I found a number of true saints who accepted me with all my muddled spiritual understanding and taught me in the Scriptures and who loved me with the love of Christ. It was a precious beginning to my life as part of the body of Christ.

In 1967, the year following my conversion, a group of young people and one of the curates from the church I attended took the long train journey up to Keswick for the annual convention. I was among them. It is the only time I have been to the Keswick Convention. Memories of walking up Skiddaw, staying in a guest house which was spartan in the extreme, talks with other young people in our party about the Lord, and the final Communion Service in the convention tent at which hundreds and hundreds were present, all crowd into my mind as I think back. I was thrilled! There was something truly wonderful for me about being in the company of so many Christians and about hearing the Scriptures preached every day. The accounts from missionaries home on furlough from all over the world also captivated my attention.

I still have in my possession the official report of that summer convention. It is somewhat brown at the edges now and some of the advertisements and articles look distinctly quaint. Amongst the speakers was the Reverend Glyn Owen, who had previously been pastor of the church in Cardiff which I was later to attend. Although I remember little about him, what I do remember is the text of his sermon: "Have mercy upon me, O God" (Psalm 51:1). Until then I had been unclear about the depth of my own sin and its consequences for the Lord Jesus Christ on Calvary. As I listened that afternoon, the Lord showed me something of the depth of the wickedness in my own heart and I cried to Him for cleansing through the blood of the Lord Jesus Christ. Spiritual truths were becoming ever more clear to me.

The very last morning of the convention was Friday. The record of the meeting can be found in the annual report I have. It was a missionary meeting and I listened to account after account of the Lord's work in various parts of the world. My soul was stirred and challenged to the depths of my being. At the end of that meeting an appeal was made for those young people seriously considering God's call on their life to stand up. I rose from my seat unaware of the assembled crowds but deeply conscious that I was expressing my commitment to the God of heaven to obey His call. The official account reads:

> "Canon Houghton called for readiness to go anywhere in the world in obedience to the Lord's constraint ... The final challenge was directed especially, however, to younger people to yield to the Lord nothing less than their lives, for His service at home or overseas. And in answer to his invitation to those willing to signify their readiness for whole-time service, in any capacity wherever He might direct, a goodly number stood up: and in prayer Canon Houghton committed them and all their future way to the Lord ...

> *I heard His call, 'Come follow!'—that was all!*
> *My gold grew dim:*
> *My soul went after Him.*
> *I rose and followed—that was all;.*
> *Who would not follow, if they heard Him call!*
>
> W. R. NEWELL"
>
> (*The Keswick Week* 1967. London: Marshall, Morgan & Scott, 1967, 153.)

As I was leaving the tent, a young woman drew me aside and told me that the previous year she too had stood in recognition of God's call to His work, and that she was now preparing to leave for foreign fields. Very soon after my conversion I had a growing awareness that the Lord was preparing a work for me outside the UK. He spoke to me through the Scriptures: "Listen, O daughter, consider, and incline your ear; forget your own people also, and your father's house; so the King will greatly desire your beauty; because He is your Lord, worship Him" (Psalm 45:10–11).

The words of Nathan Brown, nineteenth century Baptist missionary to Burma, India and Japan, sounded in my consciousness:

The voice of my departed Lord, 'Go, teach all nations!'
Comes on the night air and awakes mine ear.
Why stay I here? The vows of God are on me, and I may no longer stop
To play with shadows or pluck earthly flowers,
Till I my work have done and rendered up account.
And I will go; I may no longer doubt to give up friends
And idle hopes and every tie that binds my heart to thee my country.

It was my expectation that I would fairly quickly find myself on the overseas mission field. But that was not how it happened at all. I involved myself in missionary prayer groups and read numerous missionary books. Amongst them was a paperback that fell into my hands entitled *Three Generations of Suffering*, by Georgi Vins, a Russian pastor of an unregistered Baptist Church in Kiev. He wrote about the experiences of his parents, grandparents and himself, of faith and persecution in Soviet Russia. The book made a very profound impression on me. The needs of brothers and sisters in Christ under Soviet communism were deeply imprinted on my mind and soul. I began to seek out as much information as I could obtain about their plight. An inescapable burden of prayer took hold of me and it was with great liberty and earnestness that I began to become involved in bringing their needs before God. Each Friday, I can remember, in common with many others at that time, I would try to find a place away from work at lunchtime to pray and fast for them. They were most blessed times with the sense that the Lord Himself was giving the prayer and would answer. Many of the names of those who were in prison for the Gospel became known to me. Those who worked on secret printing presses to produce the Scriptures, at great personal cost and in circumstances of great danger, were the subject of much intercession. A prayer meeting for Eastern Europe began in my church in Cardiff about this time. Many attended and there were frequently occasions when we knew the Lord giving us prayer by his Spirit.

Several times I had been to speak to my pastor about a strong sense of call to the Lord's work. By now I was convinced that the area of that call was to Eastern Europe— at that time to all intents and purposes a closed mission field behind the Iron Curtain. It seemed there was little opportunity to pursue such a calling, but the burden remained.

I became aware quickly that there was a great need for the Scriptures and Christian literature throughout communist Eastern Europe. There was a famine for the Word of God. Often Christians would write portions of the Bible by hand or try to memorise lengthy passages in the absence of a Bible in their own personal possession. Sometimes there would only be one Bible for a large congregation, which would be shared between members. Christians faced very severe penalties for disobeying laws which insisted that children under eighteen should not go to church nor to Sunday School. Evangelism was forbidden, as were children's summer camps. Those who refused to join the youth or adult branches of the Communist Party were barred from higher education and from any significant employment path.

And so I began to enquire about missions with an interest

in taking Christian literature into Eastern Europe. Training was given and visits began; these continued over a number of years. The Lord opened up to me a number of friendships with Christians in different parts of Eastern Europe and began to show me something of the work of His hands there.

I travelled widely during those years. On one occasion I was able to visit Siberia and even to walk on frozen Lake Baikal, the deepest fresh water lake in the world, in far off Irkutsk. Strong links had been formed with Christian radio broadcasters who preached to those living in Eastern Europe. Earl Poysti was one such dear brother with whom I had come into contact and when I visited Siberia Christians there spoke with great warmth of his preaching over the radio. Through him, I came into contact with two young German/Russian women who were at that time training to present the Gospel on the radio. One of them, Susanna, who is still working for Trans World Radio, was brought up in Vorkhuta, way up in the north of Russia, within the Arctic Circle. Her father had been a pastor and the family had been exiled there. She showed me photos of their former home in Vorkhuta with snow piled high above the windows, and spoke to me of her family's experiences during those days. Once, when visiting what was then Leningrad, now St Petersburg, I can remember sitting in a cold, snowy park after a church service. An elderly lady, recognising me from the church service, came over to me and gave me some bread and tomatoes to eat. It is strange how such insignificant incidents stand out, but her gesture at the time made a big impression on me. It was not at all encouraged for Russians to have contact with Westerners, but she had very generously shared with me what she could and her smile communicated Christ to me.

Emi and Robert Poloha also worked in Christian radio and broadcast into Czechoslovakia. Their studio was in the Trans World Radio offices in Monte Carlo. Their escape with their whole family from Czechoslovakia was a miracle of the Lord's doing and they had felt God's call to radio work soon afterwards. On one visit to them, I can remember Robert going into his small radio recording cabin in the offices in Monte Carlo and saying, "And this is where I preach—and I have to imagine my congregation!" Following up some of their radio contacts in Czechoslovakia with Christian literature, we were to realise the great impact and encouragement such preaching made on those it reached.

During this time I continued to pursue an ordinary career in the UK. I trained both in adult education and as a social worker and gained growing experience in practice and in training others and in management. All the while a voice from time to time would sound in my head saying, "This is not your calling." There was no sense of disobedience in what I was doing, simply a knowledge that a day would come when things would change and I needed to be ready. I often remembered then the words of a hymn by Frances Ridley Havergal which summed up my experience:

> *Master, speak! and make me ready,*
> *When Thy voice is truly heard,*
> *With obedience glad and steady*
> *Still to follow every word.*

3

Arrival in Romania

This is the way, walk in it
(Isaiah 30:21)

I n 1989 the fall of Soviet communism astounded the
world. Millions watched on TV as the Berlin Wall was
breached and thousands upon thousands escaped to
Western Europe. The seemingly unconquerable edifice
of Soviet communism collapsed in country after country,
sometimes almost effortlessly. The Lord of Hosts, in whose
hand are all the nations of the world, had determined an end
to decades of persecution and suffering for His people and
a new day of freedom for the Gospel throughout Eastern
Europe.

I began to look for opportunities to work in Eastern
Europe. There was now no barrier to my ability to follow

God's calling in the sense of living and working in countries which had been the subject of my prayers and heart burden for so long. It was in Russia that I hoped to settle, but the Lord had other plans. By this time I was in my early forties.

Many will recall the pictures that reached our television screens soon after the collapse of communism in Romania, revealing the dreadful conditions in orphanages in that country. There was an urgent need for trained, experienced social workers from the UK to move to Romania for a period of two years to assist in the development of a programme of intervention in state orphanages. Having applied, and finding myself appointed, I prepared to leave my home and job in the UK towards the end of 1992. Looking back, it was with little sense of what awaited me that I packed my belongings.

My first sight of Bucharest was from an aeroplane at night. I peered downwards to see a very dimly lit city coming into view. The arrival was stark the airport in those days was in very poor condition and luggage was flung haphazardly on the ground in the absence of any carousel to carry the cases and bags to awaiting passengers. I was taken to an apartment in the city which was to be my home for the next months.

What followed was a real trial by fire. Those who have lived abroad will understand that the first year can be particularly difficult. A brain weariness rapidly develops as the newcomer struggles to learn a new language and adapt to a seemingly alien culture. I arrived in the midst of a harsh winter and gasped at the sight of snow blizzards the gravity of which I had never before experienced. There were frequent power shortages and I became used to arriving home to a pitch-black stairway and flat. It was not long before I realised that I was not the sole occupant of my flat—night time saw a numerous army of cockroaches put in an appearance. Shopping was a struggle as I could not make myself understood at the market and it was often difficult to find the goods which I was looking for—there were shortages of all kinds in those years immediately after the Revolution.

Bucharest still bore the scars of a city recovering from a great trauma. Many of the central buildings were pock-marked by bullet holes and shell-fire. Wreaths still lay in some of the main streets to commemorate the deaths of those who had been killed during the Revolution. The city was functioning, but in a very erratic way and without any clear sense of direction for the future. Memories of a bloody uprising were still fresh in people's memories and nobody was quite sure who could be trusted. Ceausescu's Securitate forces had been so well-established throughout the country that it was estimated that perhaps one in every three persons was linked in some way to the secret police and reported on neighbours and friends.

Sometime later I was to teach a Romanian student who had been a soldier in the Romanian army in Bucharest when the Revolution had first broken out. His account of what he had observed was fascinating. He was a young man when he had been conscripted to the army and when the Revolution broke out he had not had a great deal of experience as a soldier. On the day when Ceausescu was to give what turned out to be his final speech from the balcony of a great building overlooking Unirii Square, Petrica was on duty in that same square with a large number of other soldiers.

They had been ordered to keep a close eye on the crowd and to counter the slightest sign of any opposition. A huge number of people were gathered in the square that day. The country was in great fear, knowing that the consequences of any opposition to the regime could result in imprisonment or death, but such was the extent of suffering and hardship in the country that many began to be emboldened to the point of resisting such a punitive system. Many knew of the protests that had taken place in Timișoara.

Petrica recounted to me how he had begun to hear the slightest whisper of opposition from the assembled crowds: "Jos Ceausescu! Jos Ceausescu!" ("Down with Ceausescu! Down with Ceausescu!") At first the sound was hardly audible, but then as those gathered became bolder the sound became louder and louder, until at last it seemed that virtually the whole crowd was screaming, "Down with Ceausescu! Down with Ceausescu!" The president was in the middle of giving a speech and, as the sound of the crowd crescendoed, he lifted his head and looked around, seemingly in total disbelief at what was happening. An uncharacteristic uncertainty and hesitancy could be observed in his expression. His advisers recommended his departure. He left the balcony and not long afterwards a helicopter took off from the top of the building carrying himself and his wife, Elena, away from Bucharest.

Meanwhile the scene in the square became ever more chaotic. Dispersed amongst the crowd was a large number of secret police who began ordering the soldiers to fire on the crowd. Petrica told me that he could hear bullets whizzing past his ear, but he and his fellow soldiers decided that they were not prepared to fire on their own people. Their superiors were not giving orders to shoot, but the secret police had begun to fire indiscriminately on the assembled masses. The situation quickly erupted into violence and great fear and the crowds began to flee. The soldiers, Petrica amongst them, made haste to get back to their barracks, not knowing whether they were likely to be shot for insurrection. He told me that it was only the power and mercy of God that brought him through such a calamity.

I found myself working part of the week in the centre of Bucharest in poorly-furnished offices with a staff composed of both expatriates and Romanians. On the road the rest of the week I began to see for myself the situation in state orphanages all over the country. I was appalled and emotionally stunned by what I saw. So many memories flood back as I think back to those days. Late one night—I can remember there was a full moon and frozen snow lay on the ground—we arrived at a fairly small one-storey orphanage in an isolated location. A member of staff unlocked the door to let us in. She looked exhausted and angry. We discovered that she was the only member of staff on duty and there were about a hundred children there. They were all locked in smallish rooms along a long, dirty, malodorous corridor.

When I asked if I could go into some of the rooms she grudgingly agreed to unlock the doors. In each of the rooms children were crammed into tiny cots covered with filthy bedding and were in a state of misery and terror. One child was hiding under a blanket. I remember lifting the smelly blanket to reveal a little girl of about six, hardly recognisable as a human being, her face and body were so disfigured. She seized the blanket back to return to her hiding place.

Visiting another orphanage in a different part of the

country I discovered that a number of children had died there recently. A carpet had apparently been soaked and had been placed on one of the heaters to dry out. The fumes from the carpet were sufficiently toxic to kill some of the children.

I visited orphanage after orphanage all over Romania and became used to sights of great deprivation and suffering. The directors of such places were almost invariably quite comfortably off and held positions of some authority. They were well-disposed to foreign visitors, usually in anticipation of some lucrative return from such associations.

Life in those first months was quite lonely. Although glad to be occupied by work I knew very few people outside it. Having been given the address of a church before leaving home, I started to attend—it was a Baptist church not far from the centre of the city. Since I was able to understand very little in those early days, church attendance was more because I was glad to be with the Lord's people on His day than for any benefit I could derive from the preaching. Nobody invited me back to their home and sometimes I would walk home in tears. The effect of the suffering I was seeing almost on a daily basis, together with the lack of any Christian friend with whom to share, made it a difficult time.

The Romanian pastor of the church I was attending spoke little English, but one Sunday he managed to explain to me that there was an international service held in the same church building every Sunday afternoon. I began to attend. The congregation was made up almost exclusively of Americans who were either working in a secular capacity in Bucharest or who were missionaries. It was with great relief that I found myself in the company of other

Christians with whom I could communicate and whose preaching I could understand. An American couple from the congregation, Wayne and Pat Nauman, took me under their wing and became my very good friends. They were Baptist missionaries with experience in Christian radio work and had come to Romania at about the same time as I had to help set up Christian radio stations throughout the country. Their home was a caravan near to the studio in the city and I became a regular visitor.

Most of us in the international church were struggling with life in Romania in one way or another and it was such a help to be able to pray together and to study the Word and to help each other as much as we could. It was a small but close knit group of believers and I was so thankful to the Lord for providing me with fellowship with such people.

It was not unusual for me to find myself at the Christian radio studio when I had free time and I got to know the staff there well. A new studio was being built at the time and one often had to pick one's way through planks and cement materials to get into the studio. A thrilling opportunity to broadcast the Gospel on the radio had opened up in the country since the fall of communism and Christians wanted to make full use of this possibility.

One day there was a visitor at the studio—Pastor Iosif Ton. He had returned from exile in America immediately following the fall of Ceausescu. Previously he had been the pastor of a large Baptist church in Oradea on the other side of the country near the Hungarian border and he had written widely on Christian subjects and was well known both in Romania and in the West. I had heard him preach on several occasions in my own home church in Cardiff.

He had taken on important responsibilities with regard to the development of Christian radio in Romania and he was there to discuss some urgent matters with the staff. Pastor Ton remembered preaching in my church and we had a brief conversation. I was somewhat in awe of him.

Some months later Wayne Nauman was due to visit the new Christian radio station in Oradea. On the morning of the planned departure Pat contacted me and asked me if I would accompany them both on the long car journey to Oradea. Others were going, and the car would be very full, but she had a strong sense from the Lord that she and I should also go. She was not usually given to strong inclinations of this kind and it almost seemed out of character for her. This seemingly chance incident had such a great significance when I look back.

It was a hot day in May and we had to take it in turns to sit on the floor of the car, such was the crush inside. Eventually arriving in Oradea, we went to Pastor Ton's office. Once formal discussions had taken place about radio matters, Pat and I remained behind in the office whilst the rest of the group made their way to another meeting. We began chatting informally with Pastor Ton and he enquired about my work background and skills and qualifications and asked what had brought me to Romania. He explained that a new Bible Institute had been started in Oradea and that one of the subjects they were teaching was social work. There were so many desperate social problems in Romania following years of communism, he explained, and Christians wanted to prepare those who would be able to work in such situations, both by helping practically and by bringing the Gospel to those in great difficulty. Would I be willing to move to Oradea and teach such students? I agreed that I would. All this happened within the space of about fifteen minutes, but I had no doubt that it was from the Lord. I remember walking on my own outside afterwards, wondering at such a sudden turn of events, but with such a great peace and joy that the Lord was in this.

4

Oradea and its Students

But other seed fell on good ground
(Mark 4:8)

And so I moved to Oradea. I lived in an apartment block which was a long tram-ride from Institul Biblic Imanuel—Emmanuel Bible Institute. The city had at one time been part of Hungary and there was a sizeable minority of the population that still spoke Hungarian. There was also a large Romany population, many of whom were to be seen on the streets in flamboyant dress—the women in long, brightly coloured skirts and tops with their heads covered in scarves, whilst the men had long twirling moustaches and dressed in black hats and trousers and leather jackets. It was a beautiful sight. It was obvious from the now faded and uncared for buildings in the city centre that Oradea had known epochs of grandeur in far off days. But now most of the city was filled with communist style apartment blocks in varying stages of decay. Just outside of Oradea there was a resort with hot underground springs and sanatoria where many people came from long distances for treatment for all sorts of diseases and ailments.

I began teaching almost immediately. It is hard to describe something of the size of the task I was facing. Emmanuel Bible Institute had only recently been established. There were no proper buildings to speak of and classes were held wherever rooms were available—sometimes in part of the newly started Christian school, or in the church buildings or Sunday School accommodation. It was necessary to develop a curriculum from absolutely nothing. There were no text books and my grasp of Romanian was still extremely rudimentary. All I had was a blackboard and a piece of chalk (and sometimes not even that!) There was nobody to consult about my speciality or to assist me in the preparation.

But what the Lord did provide me with was the most extraordinary opportunity to come into contact with a large group of students whose spiritual lives impressed me profoundly. I was to discover that the city in which I was living had been the scene of a powerful revival not many years previously. Many of the students I was teaching were literally children of that revival and I heard account after account of their own first hand experiences of those times. They would tell me how the walls of the Second Baptist Church had actually shaken, so powerful was the presence of God in that place. Many recounted that there was a sense throughout the whole city that God had visited them, and those who visited the church in question were very aware of His presence in that place.

The outward result of that revival was a rapid and extensive flourishing in the growth of churches throughout the city and a great hunger after God. Very many were converted. At the beginning of the revival Liviu Olah was the pastor of the Second Baptist Church. There was a movement of great repentance amongst the leaders of that church preceding the revival. The political character of the country was still communist and restrictions and punitive measures of all kinds against the Christians were the order of the day. Liviu Olah was himself eventually exiled and subsequently Pastor Iosif Ton took over leadership of that church.

What I saw in many of my students were the direct results of that revival upon their lives. Each year I would have over a hundred students usually, but my very first class made the most lasting impression on me. One evening, soon after my arrival in Oradea, there was a knock on my door late in the evening. I opened the door to find a young woman standing there. She explained that her name was Mirela Balogh and that she was one of the students in the class. Mirela told me with joy that she and her class mates had been praying for a Christian to teach them social work and they had been told that I had arrived.

I met the class shortly afterwards. How well I recall that very day! There were only seventeen students in that class—smaller than the average number of students in a class. They were sitting on wooden benches behind old-fashioned wooden desks, staring at me with smiles full of wonder and thankfulness. A number of them were mature students. Christians had been unable to access higher education during the Ceausescu years and many had only been able to get menial employment despite their academic potential. Many were already mature in suffering also.

The most lasting impression of them was of the love of Christ expressed in their lives. I had very rarely seen Christ's love so tangibly evident. It moulded their behaviour and their characters. It was very powerful in its effect and I was later to see how this love drew others in great need to the Saviour. There was a graciousness and humility about these students and an ability to forgive and to persevere in loving even enemies. It was no wonder that I came to love them so much. The Lord had purposes for many of them of which I could hardly have dreamt at that first meeting. In His unfathomable providence God had brought me into contact with a group of men and women who were sparkling spiritual jewels. I never deserved to be the recipient of such blessing and there was nothing in my life that would have merited such a privilege. We belong to One who not only justifies the ungodly, but whose goodness and mercy follow us even when we least deserve such blessing. We are vigorously pursued by grace.

Over the years I came to know these students very well. Often they would all gather in my tiny apartment of an evening and I would buy fizzy drinks and biscuits and we would sing—it was then I first discovered that Romanians sing like the Von Trapps! We would study the Scriptures and we would pray. These men and women could pray as I had rarely heard before. Those times of fellowship were very sweet to all of us. They shared much about their lives and their knowledge of the Saviour with me and I began to realise a little of what they had already suffered.

Corina was pale-skinned and had long, untidy straight hair. She was invariably late for everything. Strong-minded and determined from a young age, she drank in everything I could teach her. Often she would arrive with a young child in tow. She explained that this was Ramona who was a young girl she was looking after. When on subsequent occasions I was to visit Corina's home, I learnt that her father was a Pentecostal pastor who had been imprisoned for the Gospel some years previously and that there were many children in her family. Corina was convinced that the Lord was calling her to work with abandoned children.

Ramona and Corina first met when Corina was regularly visiting a psychiatric institution for children in the city as a volunteer. She came upon one of the many children who never left their cots—a little girl named Ramona, who was five years old but who had not yet learnt to walk or speak. Enquiring further of the doctors about her, Corina was told "She is just a cabbage—she will never be anything else—there's no point spending time with her." If the doctor in question had but realised, that statement was the biggest possible challenge to Corina to prove him mistaken. She delights in attempting what to most ordinary mortals would appear absolutely impossible.

So she began to visit Ramona regularly and to spend time especially with her. Endless hours were spent talking to her, playing with her, taking her out of her cot and teaching her to crawl and then to walk. Ramona could see that someone loved her and she began to flourish under Corina's attention, responding eagerly to her encouragements. Quickly it became apparent that Ramona, far from being a "cabbage" had great potential. After seeking and obtaining the necessary permission, Corina began to take Ramona home to spend time with her family and, increasingly frequently, to stay overnight with them. Eventually Corina adopted her. Ramona, in time, developed into a beautiful young woman who did exceedingly well at school and became so proficient at playing the piano that she was able to give solo recitals. She was converted as a teenager. She was the first of literally hundreds of abandoned children with whom Corina subsequently worked and is still working. Corina eventually adopted four children and opened a large, beautifully equipped house for abandoned children whom she would later place in Christian foster or adoptive families. Eternity will reveal the extent to which the Lord has used this one woman for his great purposes.

Cristina spoke excellent English and was another of the students in that first class. Again, following contact with her parents, I realised that her father had suffered much under communism and that her mother had lost her job, whilst her husband had been in prison, because she was discovered helping at a secret Christian children's camp one summer. Cristina in later years went on to pursue doctoral studies in social work and then to teach on the social work course at what, in later years, became known as the Christian University of Oradea.

During their final year some of the students in this class began to talk about setting up a Christian social work agency in the city, to bring the Gospel to a great number of young and older people in need and to try to meet their needs in a practical way. Students like Mirela and Estera had a growing conviction that this was something that should happen. It seemed beyond the realms of human possibility to begin thinking about such a new vision. There were no available resources to speak of, with the exception of a small number of poverty-stricken students. However, the conviction increased and the Christian agency, CASA, began as soon as they graduated and continues to this day, reaching more people than we could ever have dreamed of.

Marinela had worked in earlier years as a nurse in a large psychiatric institution. She could remember times when patients would be given literally a handful of tablets to sedate them and would then be forced to sit in rows, watching interminable speeches from Ceausescu on television. She and Mirela could remember how they would often break the rules of the hostel where they were staying and creep out furtively on a Sunday to hear Iosif Ton preach at the Baptist church—it was forbidden for student nurses to attend a church of any kind at the time. Marinela knew that the Lord was calling her to work with people who were dying. Although as a young woman she was outwardly slight and even frail looking, Marinela is tenacious of spirit and walks very closely with the Lord. She went on to establish a great hospice work in the city of Oradea which now employs a sizeable staff group and has reached untold numbers with practical medical and social help when they are dying, but also with the Gospel.

Her mother became a Christian when she was expecting Marinela. There was a Christian family that lived next door to them. Marinela's mother had heard them singing Christian hymns and she gladly accepted their invitation to go to church with them. Marinela enjoyed going to church with her mother as a little girl. When she was eight years old there was a revival in Oradea. They needed to leave their village at 5am by train to get to church in Oradea in time. To have any chance of getting in to the church meant arriving there two hours early. It was already full by the time they used to arrive. In those days there was only one small church building and the balcony was always full to overflowing. Even as a child of eight Marinela felt God's presence filling the place. A longing arose in her to go to that church as often as possible. There had been problems in the church prior to the revival—deacons drinking alcohol after church in a nearby bar and also some who worked on a collective farm who used to steal produce from the collective to take home. Brother Olah, the pastor whom God used greatly in that revival, had a heart full of compassion for those who were not saved. In 1974 he called the members of the Second Baptist Church in Oradea to prayer and repentance. He realised that the Christians needed to repent before sinners would be saved.

Marinela started to pray every day that God would let her move to Oradea and go to that church. She used to pray for Brother Olah every day and for her father who was not saved. She understood clearly what sin was and what salvation was, even though she was not yet converted herself. She promised God that if He would let her come to live in Oradea she would serve him all the days of her life.

In 1977 Pastor Liviu Olah was exiled to America and Brother Iosif Ton came to be the pastor. Then Marinela started to pray for Pastor Ton as well. She still longed to go to that church regularly and prayed about it every day. She also wanted to go to the high school where it was possible to train to become a nurse, but there was fierce competition to get into that school. The morning of the entrance exam her mother asked her what subject she would like for the exam if she could choose. Marinela told her, and that very subject came up in the exam. She came third amongst all those who sat the exam, and knew that God had answered her prayer.

Marinela, now converted, started to pray that God would show her how He wanted her to serve Him. She was baptised on 7 June 1981 along with about sixty others, including her brother. Her mother had a close work colleague she had invited to the baptism who had never been to church before. After the service the colleague said that she wished she had never come to the baptism. Marinela asked her why and she said that it was because now she knew that if she did not repent and seek baptism she would have to give an account at the throne of judgement at the last day. After that she used to visit them every day to listen to cassettes of preaching from Brother Olah or Pastor Ton. She was very moved by the preaching, and just before Pastor Ton left for America she came to church again. She wanted to hear him one last time and she asked her husband's permission to come.

At the end of the service Pastor Ton said a new convert who was disabled wanted to be baptised. It was the pastor's last Sunday in the church before he had to leave for America and this brother wanted to be baptised before his departure. Immediately she heard this, the work colleague said that she too wanted to be baptised that day. Pastor Ton realised that she had truly been converted and agreed to baptise her that day. She had lots of problems afterwards with her husband and at work because of her conversion. Her sister-in-law was a strong communist and was also the head of the section where Marinela's mother and her friend worked. She sent the Securitate to Marinela's house as a result of the woman's conversion. Her mother faced lots of questions because she had taken her work colleague to church. The lady is still in the church and is in her seventies. Her daughter was in the same school as Marinela and used to come to church with her—her father used to follow them to see where they were going. She was converted too.

After leaving high school Marinela worked in a psychiatric hospital for a while as a nurse and for eight years in the haematology department of another hospital. Many used to die there from leukaemia and it was a heartbreaking experience to see relatives sobbing for a long time in the corridor after somebody they loved had died and nobody would comfort them or help them.

After 1989 everything changed. For years Marinela had longed to study theology and suddenly this became a real possibility when the Institul Biblic Imanuel opened in Oradea. She was accepted amongst the first intake of students. One of the doctors in the hospital encouraged her before she left to come back once she had trained. He would look after the patients' bodies and she would take care of their souls. His comment kept coming back to her when she was training. I was her teacher and told her of the growth of the hospice work in the West. In 1994 she had the chance to visit the UK for the first time and saw some of the hospice care work first-hand.

During her last year at Bible College a letter from England arrived asking if one of the students would be prepared to work for a number of weeks in the summer in a hospice in Braşov—it was the first hospice in the country. All her colleagues convinced her that the letter was for her, because they all knew of her longing to work with people who were dying. Marinela went to Braşov that summer. After the very first visit she made to someone whom the hospice was supporting, she stayed awake all night praying and rejoicing because she knew for certain that this was the work to which God had called her. But when the time in Braşov was finished she explained to those there that she needed to go back to Oradea to start a hospice work there.

Marinela spoke with Pastor Paul Negrut about her conviction, and he said that he would look for some financial support for such a work from the UK. It was to be called Emmanuel hospice and would be under the auspices of the Emmanuel Church in Oradea. Marinela came into contact with a female Christian doctor who was willing to help in the work. They prayed together every day about the matter. They waited, but no word came about financial support, so one day they decided that, with or without support, it was time to start. They met at a tram-stop in town for their first work meeting. Marinela had obtained a list of thirty cancer patients in need of palliative care from the oncological hospital and they started visiting them that day. They had no resources of any kind when they started. She had used all her money to buy a season ticket for the tram so that she could visit the patients in their homes, and her mother had given her enough food to last a while. After about a week they received their first gift of syringes and medical equipment and then eventually began to have salaries.

One of the very first patients with whom Marinela worked was Virgil, an eleven-year-old boy. She began to visit him in hospital as part of the practice necessary for the course she was following. Virgil was suffering from leukaemia and in those days most children who contracted leukaemia in Romania would die. He came from an Orthodox family background but, while in hospital in Cluj, he had been given a children's Bible by some Christians who were visiting. Sometimes I would visit Virgil with Marinela and this Bible could always be seen open on his pillow. With great animation and interest Virgil used to tell about what he had read in that Bible. He understood clearly why the Lord Jesus had come to earth and he knew that his sins had been forgiven because of the Cross. His trust in God was strong and evident to all those around him. One evening, there was a terrible storm and there were no staff around. The children in his ward were all very frightened and Virgil gathered them around him and they knelt down while he prayed for God's protection for them all.

Little by little Virgil became weaker and it was clear that he was dying. Marinela had many opportunities to speak to him about heaven and Virgil's eager anticipation of seeing the Lord was constant and real. Eventually he died and went to be with the Lord. Outwardly, his life could have been judged as almost without significance, but he was to be the first-fruits of a great work of God. There were others in that class in the Bible Institute who went on to be much used of God in pioneering works. How little were we aware of that at the time! Whenever I think back to that first class, it always seems to me that they were God's hundredfold: "But he who received seed on the good ground is he who hears the word and understands it, who indeed bears fruit and produces: some a hundredfold ..." (Matthew 13:23).

5

Revival and its Effects

... that the word of the Lord may run swiftly and be glorified
(2 Thessalonians 3:1)

As my grasp of the language began to improve, I began to derive more and more benefit from the church services I was attending. In those days the congregation used to crowd into the old church building. There were two services each Sunday morning to accommodate all those who wished to attend, and at either service it was important to be there well before the service began in order to have a seat on one of the wobbly wooden benches that filled the church building. Each bench would be filled with worshippers, and the aisles and the back of the church would also be packed with those who were standing.

The services would continue for two or three hours but nobody seemed to mind having to stand for such a long time.

On one occasion, Liviu Olah, who had been pastor of the church when the revival broke out, returned from America to preach. I had never seen so many people in the church. I managed to find a tiny standing space at the back of the church and I can remember thinking at the time that if someone in the congregation were to faint because of the heat, the crowd was packed so tightly that they would not have fallen to the ground.

There were times when the Lord drew very near to us as we worshipped. Although I was there after the revival occurred, compared with church life at home it was as if the revival were still continuing. One Easter there was a joint service with the Hungarian Baptist church in the city. There were racial tensions between the Romanians and the Hungarians and this kind of joint service did not occur very often. However I can recall the presence of God very powerfully at that service, both in the preaching from Hungarian and Romanian pastors, but also in the sense that we felt the love of God shed abroad in our hearts in a most remarkable way.

During a communion service one Sunday there was such an awareness of the Lord's presence that one felt as if the roof of the church had been lifted and heaven had come down. In Oradea I often listened to the preaching of Iosif Ton and Paul Negrut. There was an awesome authority to the Word preached and many were convicted of sin and converted. At one evangelistic meeting in the large new church which was subsequently built, where over 3000 people would have been present, Paul Negrut preached from

Jonah. We could have listened all night and nobody wanted him to stop. When he finished preaching there was total quiet in the vast congregation for some moments, followed by the sound of weeping all around the building as men and women repented and sought the Saviour.

On one occasion Iosif Ton preached a series of messages on being changed into the image of Christ. It is difficult to describe the effect of those messages. We thronged to listen, and with great joy we received the preached Word. It was as though something of the glory of Christ was revealed to us and we longed for a deeper knowledge of this most powerful Saviour. We could not forget how the Lord had met with us in such preaching and we hungered for more. There were also many times when the Word convicted us so powerfully of our sin that we had to cry to him for forgiveness and cleansing.

Many members of the congregation used to meet for prayer at 5am each morning. In the vestibule of the old church were many black-and-white photographs of baptisms, often carried out in secret very early in the morning under the former regime. When I looked at these photographs I was always moved by the bravery and boldness of those who had stood firm for the Lord under great opposition. I heard so many stories from different individuals about the suffering of recent times. Two of the pastors in the church I attended spoke of times when they had to attend the infamous headquarters of the Securitate in the city each week. They were invariably interrogated and beaten and then would preach again in the church the following Sunday. Whilst they were being interrogated, a group of brothers and sisters from the church would stand outside all the time, praying—which was in itself a punishable act. The pastors said that the prayers of those people were exceedingly precious to them.

A pastor spoke to the student congregation at the Bible Institute of a time when his electricity supply was connected to the water supply in the hope that he would be electrocuted. I heard of another faithful pastor who had been killed by electrocution under the guise of an unfortunate accident. It was not unknown for Christians to be killed in road accidents which had been pre-planned by the Securitate. One pastor told me that his teenage daughter at one time had been kidnapped by the Securitate and they had threatened to rape her. He said that of all the trials this had been the hardest. His daughter was eventually returned to him unharmed.

The year that I left Oradea my final-year students were facing some oral exams from outside examiners. These visitors came from a Hungarian university in the city. As with any teacher, I knew my students well and there is a sense in which it is usually possible to anticipate the kind of results they are likely to achieve in exams. I was invited to be present at the oral examination. Those examining the social work students had no qualifications or experience in social work—they were qualified in sociology. The examination began and I was horrified. Most of the students knew their subject matter very well, but they were given appallingly low marks or were failed outright. A few students, whom I knew to be amongst the least able, were given high marks. Individual students became the butt of ridicule and outright scorn, all quite unjustly. During the middle of the examining, I was so concerned at what was happening that I went to speak to Paul Negrut. Looking very concerned he explained to me that there were a number of factors operating behind the scenes. In addition to the latent tensions between Romanians and Hungarians there was envy on the examiners' part at the relatively good conditions the Bible Institute was able to offer in comparison with their own context. Furthermore, there was an unseen but very real opposition to the Gospel and for everything the Bible Institute represented. He advised me to remain silent and to pray. I returned to the examination hall to witness the continuing verbal assault on my students.

Afterwards, I spoke to a number of those students individually. Their reactions amazed me. Far from being full of indignation as I was, they spoke of their trust in a God who was sovereign and who would finally judge righteously. They were able to praise Him with their whole hearts even in the midst of such injustice, the implications of which were so potentially damaging for them. I had learnt much about God's sovereignty in years that had gone by, but here I was seeing an experiential trust in this God in circumstances of great difficulty.

Again and again I was to witness this same faith in God's sovereignty. On one occasion I accompanied a student on her practice visit to an elderly couple, both of whom were very ill. As soon as we arrived it was apparent that their situation was one of great hardship and trial. Before we left the husband wanted to pray and he insisted on struggling to his feet to do so. What followed from both husband and wife were prayers full of praise to a God they clearly knew intimately and whom they trusted absolutely.

Many of my students had had profound experiences of

God's work in their lives and a deep conviction of sin before they were converted. Daniel told me that he could remember being so convicted of his need of repentance during a church service that he knelt down in the aisle and cried out to God to save him. It was so important to him to find God's forgiveness that he cared not in the slightest what others might think of him.

They were thrilling days to be living through despite the outward dullness of daily life in many ways. I had heard that, before the Revolution, Pastor Iosif had been walking in fields on the outskirts of Oradea when the Lord had given him a conviction that in that very city, which was then so much under Communist oppression, there would be a Christian radio station, a Christian printing press and a Christian university. Each of these seemed totally improbable—it was forbidden to listen to Christian broadcasts on the radio, Christian literature of any kind was in very short supply and Christians were not allowed access to higher education as a general rule. However, each of these became a reality during the days in which I lived there. In the very city in which I was living, Christian radio had been established, a Christian printing press set up and what was eventually to become a Christian university was started.

New-found freedom to share the Gospel with others was precious to Christians and there was a great interest in spiritual matters in the community at large. Students would often give out tracts to everybody on a tram. In contrast to reactions in the UK, everybody would then be seen eagerly reading the contents of the tract and usually none would be thrown away.

One Christmas I stayed with a large family. As was the

custom on Christmas Eve there would be carol singing from house to house throughout the night, with food offered liberally en route. I accompanied them on their singing tour and at about 2am we arrived in the middle of a large housing estate. We were surrounded by a circle of high-rise blocks of flats, with hardly a light to be seen in any of them. Standing in some trepidation, I wondered about the wisdom of arousing an entire neighbourhood in the middle of the night with our singing. Such carol singing had been forbidden under the former regime. The family I was accompanying had the most beautiful voices; the father would start singing and then conduct his family with great enthusiasm through a recital of amazing proportions. The words of Romanian Christmas carols, as for so many carols in different languages, present the Gospel with a wonderful clarity.

Following the father's cue we began to sing. The most beautiful harmonies sounded out into the darkness of that snowy night and the words gave us much joy as we thought about the One who had left the glory for us and "though He was rich, yet for your sakes he became poor" (2 Corinthians 8:9). After a few moments lights went on in flat after flat around the blocks which encircled us. More and more lights were switched on as we continued singing, and people began to open their shutters and lean out of their windows to listen. It was an unforgettable night. Far from causing the slightest disquiet, it was obvious that those listening were very glad indeed of the opportunity to listen to the carols and we prayed as we sang that the words would truly reach their hearts.

There was an eagerness amongst most Christians to speak

of the Lord when they met. He was the never-ending focus of their conversations. Of course, they did speak of other things, but somehow the discussion would come back to Him—what He was teaching them, how He had spoken to them, how much there was for which to praise Him and how amazing was the grace He had shown us. It was no wonder then that so many of those conversations ended in prayer. I missed that spontaneous fellowship in conversation when I came home. Sometimes it seemed to me that we could talk of anything else but not of the Lord. Our conversation reflects the preoccupation of our hearts and will indicate where our true treasure is to be found.

A passionate urgency to reach those who had not heard the Gospel also characterised those times. It was for this reason that the Bible Institute set up a school of social work. There was a determination to try to reach those who had somehow slipped off the edge of society—street children and abandoned children; people who were dying; men, women and children with disabilities; those who had spent long, seemingly wasted years in institutions. As in the nineteenth century in Great Britain, following the great revival of the eighteenth century, there was a God-given call to reach such people with the Gospel. Similarly in Romania, the spiritual work was closely followed by practical social consequences. And I witnessed the Lord Himself calling, preparing and raising up those who would pioneer such works. It was a work of His right hand.

6

A Visit to Moldova

I will give you the treasures of darkness
(Isaiah 45:3)

Among the students I taught at Oradea there had always been a small number from the Republic of Moldova. They had impressed me in a number of ways. Without exception, they were always the poorest of the students I taught. I can remember one of them, Lidia, praying for needed pencils in order to write. The Moldovan students were also those who seemed to have the most severe health problems—they had all had tuberculosis at one time or another. Two of my former Moldovan students have already died at an early age. In spite of, or because of, this they made an impression on me as men and women of great faith, often born out of much suffering. Another of them was Veronica Pozdirca. By 1997 I had left Oradea and was working for a Christian charity in the UK. I met Veronica again "coincidentally" when we were both visiting Oradea at the same time. She asked me to visit her country of Moldova to help her. Her request lodged in my mind and would not go away.

Some time later, in the early months of 1998, I found myself on board a large, distinctly ancient plane flying through a blizzard to Chişinău, the capital of Moldova. How well I remember that first visit! There were just fifteen passengers with plenty of space in a large plane. At the time there was a common joke that only the Mafia and missionaries flew to Moldova—a glance at my fellow passengers indicated that this may not have been too far from the truth! I had almost missed my connection at Schiphol airport in Amsterdam, as the airport staff insisted that I could not get into Moldova without an invitation, which I did not possess. My name was called on the tannoy system with disturbing regularity. Eventually, but reluctantly, I was allowed to board, with warnings that I might not be allowed to enter Moldova on arrival. After running a great distance through the airport, clothed in heavy sheepskin and boots, to catch my Air Moldova plane, I watched as the weather began to close in. Feeling suddenly quite alone I prayed that God would go before me. There is a secret place of the Most High where we can have fellowship with Him whom our souls love in every time of need, and it was to that place that I resorted.

There were no overhead lockers on the plane and the safety instructions were dealt with very perfunctorily by a well-built Russian-looking air hostess. Reading the flight magazine on board I discovered that the Director General of Air Moldova was twenty-six years old and enjoyed playing billiards. Passengers were assured, in strange English, that "our company rests on three whales: flight safety, high level of service and profitability." The following statement, that "we have difficult times ahead of us: we need to invest into renovation of our flying stock and into purchasing a new one" somehow did not instil the same degree of confidence.

The plane arrived late in the evening and I can recall very few lights over the capital as we came in to land between two high walls of snow on the runway. We disembarked through the underside of the plane and our small group seemed to disappear in different directions into the dark and icy cold. Unsure where to go I wandered towards what I thought was an airport terminal building. The building was poorly lit and cold, and luggage was lying on the floor in disorderly fashion. The airport has since been rebuilt, but in those days it was little more than a large shed. Having paid for my visa, and realising that my luggage had not made the journey with me, I was giving a description of my case to a woman official. Suddenly Veronica was beside me and how we rejoiced to see one another again! It proved to be the beginning, in God's remarkable purposes, of the most incredible venture of faith. But at the time I could barely see one step ahead.

A suicidally-fast drive into town inducted me into the *modus operandi* of Moldovan travel. Heavy snow was falling onto already thick snow. We arrived at a tall, crumbling block of flats and negotiated our way through a very dark entrance into a tiny lift and were soon being welcomed very warmly into a small flat by Anea and her adopted daughter,

Galina. Little did I know at the time what a vital part they were to play in my life.

Those first days were busy and crammed full of all sorts of early impressions. There were lots of similarities I could see with life in Romania. Many people spoke Romanian, but with a strong Russian accent and lots of Russian words thrown in so that I sometimes struggled to understand. The food was not dissimilar to the food to which I had become accustomed in Romania, although it was poorer and meal times seemed to be more erratic. A number of my new friends obviously felt a great affinity with Romania and things Romanian.

And yet there were differences: Chișinău felt more distinctly Russian than Romanian to me, with its Soviet-style government buildings and parks that reminded me of Russia—huge snow-laden firs, grandchildren with tight hold of their grandmother's hand wandering slowly through broad tree-lined avenues, and men and women encased in huge fur hats, apparently oblivious to the temperature. Anea's Bible was in Romanian, though written in Cyrillic script. Street signs had newly been changed, replacing former Soviet names, like Lenin Street or Komsomol Avenue, with names that reflected Romanian and Moldovan history. Although I had lived in Romania for the years immediately following the Revolution, when the country was still experiencing some turmoil and instability, there seemed to be a greater harshness to day-to-day life here in Moldova. Life seemed to be very hard for most people.

Trips on public transport stood out for their theatrical sense of the ridiculous. Small minibuses hurled themselves through the city at frenzied speeds, with occupants crushed together to the point of asphyxiation in a pick-pocket's paradise. Their drivers often drove in a crazed fashion, choosing the shortest distance between any two points, regardless of obstacles in the form of other cars. The traffic police had an ominous presence and drivers were very used to offering the expected bribe to rid themselves of just or unjust accusations. One became aware of Mafia influences quickly—there was an early experience of being forced off the road by a blacked-out Mafia car which ignored every traffic rule. I learnt that human-trafficking was, and is, a very big problem in Moldova, in which the Mafia plays a significant role. Sometimes I would see young women in the city or at the airport dressed in uncharacteristically expensive clothes and sporting designer bags and wonder about the source of their seeming wealth. Their eyes and their expressions often had a desolate look.

So many people were leaving this little country. I became aware that whole generations of families had left, or were preparing to leave, usually for America. And they did not return other than for short visits. Many Christians, including pastors, were leaving, and the Moldovan Christians who remained said that they were changed when they returned. They had lost their spiritual fire. They spoke of houses and possessions and new cars and a bright future, and they visited armed with video cameras to take back films of church life in the old country—but their passionate pursuit of the Saviour had dimmed. That is what people said.

Later, on future visits, I often saw something of this exodus first-hand. There would not be room to move in the airport very early in the morning. A multitude of pilgrims were leaving for the promised land of America. It reminded

me of photos I had seen of people migrating to the United
States at the beginning of the twentieth century. Elderly
women were sitting in the airport looking bereft and
disorientated. I can see one such person now, in my mind's
eye. Her belongings lay at her feet—the fruit of a lifetime's
work in a few large carrier bags tied with string. A scarf
covered her head and she had no outer coat, only a well-worn
cardigan and a skirt in faded colours that was frayed and
old. Her high-coloured complexion and her swollen, rough
hands indicated the years she would have spent working on
the land. Her grandchildren played excitedly around her.
I saw no husband and speculated that she was probably a
widow. Her sons and daughters-in-law, dressed in their best
clothes, were talking animatedly to officials who were trying
to ensure that this great wave of migrants had completed
all the right papers. The men-folk were wearing black
leather caps and their pockets were bulging with documents
needed to make this great transition to another world.
Relatives would have written, encouraging them in this most
momentous of decisions and speaking of warmer climes, a
good education for the children and opportunities for those
prepared to work hard.

On one occasion I witnessed several generations of a
Christian family leaving for Sacramento in California. The
group included a man who had been leader of the choir in a
big church for many years. The choir and scores of members
of the congregation had come to see him and his family off.
They assembled in formation and filled the airport with the
most wonderful sound of Moldovan Christian hymns, sung
in many parts and at great volume. A pastor led in prayer
for those leaving, with a voice that resonated throughout

the airport. Passers-by looked bemused. As the time came to depart, the great crowd of those leaving separated from those remaining. There were very many tears and hugs and final Christian greetings: "Cu Domnul"—"May the Lord go with you." And yet another family left.

The spiritual life of the Moldovans I got to know impressed me a great deal. I came to know Christians whose lives were saturated with God. Veronica was one such person. She was teaching at the Bible College and I could see what a splendid teacher she was becoming and what a powerful example of Christ's love and power she was. Her students loved her. On the day after I first arrived Veronica told me that she was meeting with some young women at the church and asked if I would go with her. I gladly agreed and at the end of the afternoon we arrived at an outbuilding of the church, having walked a long distance through ice-packed snow.

We arrived in a room which seemed as cold as a fridge. It was barely furnished, but had some chairs. One by one young women started arriving. I met Angela who was in her early twenties and had spent most of her life in institutions or on the streets. Many of her teeth were missing. She spoke loudly and was poorly dressed. I learnt that for months after meeting Veronica she had made her life difficult; she had often been aggressive towards her and had, on one memorable afternoon, put a large quantity of snow down Veronica's back! But Angela had become a Christian through Veronica's consistent witness to a Saviour who seeks out the lost and the hopeless of this world. More women arrived—a young mother and her child who had been living on the streets; a number who had spent their young lives in state "care" and were now living in hostels, but barely surviving; a young woman called Lena who had also been converted through Veronica and who wanted to train to be a hairdresser. Within an hour the room was full. A time of simple Bible study and sometimes rumbustious discussion, enthusiastic, but not always tuneful singing, and fervent prayer began. It was very moving. After a couple of hours the women took their leave reluctantly, each taking a parcel of food Veronica had prepared for them.

The more time I spent with Veronica, the more I became aware of a life that was given over to her Lord. She spoke about Him to so many and her life was being spent out for Him. I can remember her meeting a nephew and his wife on a trolleybus and warning them most seriously of their plight without Jesus Christ and pointing to Him most clearly. She was a woman of much prayer and much action. I remembered that, as a student, she had shared with me that she had failed to complete her schooling. She had lived in a village and her parents were believers and the local church used to meet in their house. As a consequence both parents and children were hounded by the communist authorities. Veronica had been beaten so many times at school for being a Christian that she could not bear to go to school any longer and had left prematurely. She had taken up dress-making but, after the Revolution, was chosen as one of the first Moldovan students to be given the opportunity to train at a new Christian Bible College in Romania.

One day she asked me if I would like to join her in visiting a closed institution for women and girls with disabilities. I expressed my interest and we decided to go—it was the first visit for both of us. A Christian brother from the Bible College drove us the sixty kilometres to the place in question. It was a bright, sunny day with huge quantities of snow enveloping the vineyards which lined our journey. Our driver provided us with a most thrilling account of his life whilst we travelled. He had been dying from meningitis and his body had become paralysed. God had met with him in a remarkable way at the time and he had been completely restored overnight. His sixty-year-old brother had been converted as a result of having seen the Lord's work in his brother's life.

We entered a small, rather shabby town and drove through it and began to climb a hill on the other side of the town. Three large, low buildings came into view and we arrived at some tall, iron gates which barred our entrance to this closed institution. Finally, when we had satisfied the guard on duty that we were expected visitors, the gates were swung open and we drove in. The buildings were greatly in need of repair and a coat of paint. There were a small number of individuals, some with obvious learning or physical disabilities, walking around in an aimless fashion outside. Some looked very apprehensive as we approached. A few raised their arms to prevent themselves from anticipated attack or, conversely, menacingly approached us with sticks. I was not unused to such places. Whilst working in Romania I had had much contact with a whole range of institutions where adults and children lived, frequently in appalling conditions, particularly in the early years after the Revolution. But there was something that etched itself on my soul about this place. The Director met us. He had worked there for thirty-one years. One wondered what he had witnessed during that time. We had been warned that there was a good deal of corruption and lack of organisation, but we were given permission to look around and to speak to staff and those who lived there.

A number of the staff looked harsh. We discovered that they had not been paid for seven months. They did not leave their jobs because it would have been virtually impossible to find other work, and because there was always the faint hope that the salary would eventually arrive. As we walked down the stairs to the basement level we were met by an overpowering stench. Row after row of beds were crammed together in damp, malodorous rooms. Girls were lying on soiled bedding in filthy clothing. Some had the most enormous heads because of untreated encephalitis and were clearly very distressed and in great pain. There were so many thin bodies. Mostly, they lay listlessly, not having the energy to respond to any display of interest. Some of those who were not quite so ill made a feeble attempt to respond to our attentions.

We went upstairs and entered cold, dark "classrooms" where pathetic groups of children had prepared a song or a poem for the rare visitors. They performed in robotic, distressing fashion. Some appeared to collapse from the effort afterwards. As the few staff talked with one another in the corridor and left us with the girls, many gathered round us begging for food. Many seized hold of us and clamoured for eye-contact or any gesture of interest.

On that first visit, we were aware that there were a number of older women also living there, but at that time it was the children who preoccupied our attention. We had brought a small amount of clothing to distribute, but we realised that this probably would not remain in the possession of the children for very long.

As we left, it was with a sense of being completely overwhelmed at what we had seen and heard. But we were not able to forget those things.

7

An Institution in the South

... able to save to the uttermost
(Hebrews 7:25)

Veronica and I began to pray. I quickly realised that the prayer-life of my new Moldovan friends was something to be reckoned with. It was the pivot for all their actions and it permeated their day to day living. I saw people who had no resources of their own on which to depend looking to a God who had made heaven and earth, and in whose hands was all power. And they had no difficulty believing that He could do the impossible. This had been their experience. They expected great things of Him and they attempted great things for Him. And how they sought Him and pleaded His promises before Him! "Call to Me, and

I will answer you, and show you great and mighty things, which you do not know" (Jeremiah 33:3).

It was clear to us that we had to do something—that walking away from the institution we had visited and doing nothing was not an option. So visits began—at first these were just once a month. At this time I was still working in the UK and visiting Moldova as often as I could, but soon I finished work there and concentrated my energies on Moldova. It was obvious that practical help was needed, so we took food and clothing and we started some activities—games and singing—and shared simple Bible stories with the women and girls. Most of all we started to get to know a number of those who lived there. And what a joy that became!

Fast forward to November 2007. Liliana, my close colleague and friend in the work, and I are standing in the office of the formidable Director of this same institution. It is almost ten years since we first started visiting. The old Director has been removed and replaced by a new female Director. When we first visited there were about 120 women and girls living there. Now there were over three hundred. Thanks to help from international aid agencies the physical conditions in the institution have, at least superficially, improved. Many of the women have become our very dear friends. We have seen a remarkable work of God in this place.

The Director screamed at us. Think Queen of Hearts in *Alice Through the Looking Glass* and you have the slightest glimpse of the ferocity with which she is accosting us. It was a volcanic verbal explosion that lasted almost two and half hours. We stood for most of it and we said very little—the Director hardly paused for breath and did not, in any event, intend to listen to us. "You have filled these women's heads with God and the Bible! How dare you baptise them without my permission! I will not allow you to lay another finger on one more of my women here—from today you will be forbidden access here any further. You are not wanted here and we do not need you!"

By the end of the outburst, the speaker was purple with rage and one felt that a sudden heart attack was a real possibility. There had been a lot of time for reflection and silent prayer during the harangue. I thought much about the verses in Revelation which say of the Lord Jesus, "He who has the key of David, He who opens and no one shuts, and shuts and no one opens" (Revelation 3:7). It was clear to me that despite what the Director thought about her own power and authority (and she had no mean view of these) it was not at her determining that the doors to this place had opened, nor would it be if they were to shut. That was in the sovereign hand of Another.

There had also been lots of time to think about damage to reputation and personal pride. She had said some dreadful things about us. But my quiet conclusion was that it did not matter a whit what others said about us ultimately. We served another King, one Jesus, and He would judge righteously. There would be a day, when He would own our worthless name before His Father's face. We did not need to vindicate ourselves.

But I was also aware that Satan was very angry at God's work in this place. It was clear that He was stirring up this woman, who had previously given us her time and support most kindly, to such an extent that she could not control her rage in our presence. Her anger went beyond human understanding and was certainly not justified by the things that had happened, other than in spiritual terms.

So what had been happening in the intervening years?

The visits had quickly become weekly ones and the sixty-kilometre journey became a very familiar one. Anea became our driver and negotiated every pothole in the road with accuracy and speed. Usually we would go on a Saturday. It was Anea's day off from the factory, and it always seemed that there were few staff around and the girls and women had little to do then. One of the Christian songs we taught the women back in those early days included the word "joy" several times in the chorus. It was not long before a large group of women would come running to the gates as we arrived, shouting "Bucurie a venit!"—literally, "Joy has arrived!" They meant it, I think, as short-hand for the chorus they enjoyed singing, but it took on a symbolic significance for us. We had been praying that the Lord Jesus Christ Himself would bring something of the joy of His presence to this desolate place.

Often at night I would think of the girls and women who lived there and imagine their circumstances. Rejected by their families, isolated and shut off from the outside world, coping with disabilities without any of the supports which would be available in our country, suffering cold and hunger and sometimes cruelty. And I would pray. I would pray that the Lord Jesus Himself would walk among them and fill their thoughts, and even their dreams, with His presence and that they would experience His powerful love for them. The burden to pray for them became an immoveable one.

It was such a delight to get to know some of the women well. But our hearts also grieved for them when we began to understand more of the suffering that was contained in their short lives. Dorina was in her early twenties and had sustained a brain injury in a bad car accident, which had left her in a wheelchair, with restricted movement and very poor speech. She was intelligent and talkative but had been taken to the institution by her parents after the accident. Her mother was working in Italy and saw her only rarely. Her parents had divorced. Dorina would sit outside in her wheelchair in all weathers, even when the snow was on the ground. She preferred this to the noise and chaotic neglect of life indoors. At mealtimes, I remember seeing her often struggling to eat without assistance and screaming with frustration when some of the more aggressive women would steal her soup bowl and she was helpless to do anything about it. I took to feeding her when I was there, to try to ensure that she got something to eat. She showed an early interest in spiritual things. On one visit she grabbed my sleeve and started speaking with a loud voice. Struggling to understand, I realised that she was praying—thanking God for how He had worked in her life. We gave her a Bible which she kept safely under her pillow. Many times she begged us to take her from there.

Vera was not sure exactly how old she was, but we guessed she was probably in her late twenties. She had lived in this place for years and had an "artful dodger" capacity to find any food that was going—her pockets would be stuffed with an assortment of pieces of stale bread and the odd syringe. She had a very loud voice and knew everybody and was the constant source of information about everything that was happening. She would always appear wherever we were and demand attention. Her eyesight was very poor and she walked with a pronounced limp. Her temper sometimes got the better of her and she would storm off in a great fit of pique. Vera listened with great interest to the singing and to the Bible teaching and she told us she had started praying.

Always she was full of questions. "Will I get a new body when I die?" "How do I know that my sins are forgiven?" "Will you take me out of here—I want to live with Christians?" The day arrived when Vera and a small number of women about her age were, without warning, put into a bus and taken to a most dreadful institution for adults at the other end of the country. It was miles from anywhere in a very isolated location. Residents usually remained there until they died. Vera and her friends hated the new place. Within a few days they determined to make their escape and somehow negotiated the journey back to their former "home" using their wits. They walked endless miles and hitched lifts whenever they could. They were in a truly pitiable state by the time they returned and no-one could believe that they had succeeded in such a venture. But they were allowed to stay.

Lilia was blind. Again, she was unsure of her age, but we thought she was probably in her early thirties. Most days she would wander from room to room, seeking out people she knew. The lay-out of the large building was familiar to her. Staff paid her very little attention. Lilia could not remember how long she had been there, nor how or why she had arrived. She was very thin, but had the most beautiful smile and her face lit up when she knew that we were close by and she would call out our names urgently. Lilia loved the Lord. She knew the Scriptures well and delighted to listen to the messages from a Christian radio station on a radio which we had purchased for her. The radio was kept constantly in one of her pockets and she was often to be seen holding it to her ear. One day she asked me to speak to a mutual friend: "Tell him that I am not on the broad way. I am on the narrow way."

We soon started to hold a summer "camp". How different this was from the camps we may think of in our own country! We held the camp at the end of each summer and day by day would help women and girls into the field adjoining the institution, where we had prepared a barbecue and games and where we enjoyed singing and Bible stories. For some it was a very rare opportunity to get out of the room where they spent their entire lives. The weather was usually hot, so they would sit down on blankets under the dappled shade of the trees. A stranger would have thought it a peculiar gathering, perhaps. Many of the women and girls had serious physical and mental disabilities. Their clothing was poor and often smelly. The food always disappeared in record time. When we played games, limbs moved in uncoordinated fashion and there were shrieks of delight as the winner was announced. There was a lot of laughing. Sometimes we had to interrupt fights.

Someone would play the guitar and we would sing at the top of our voices until we were hoarse. The flannelgraph board came out and we used our most animated story-telling approach to share wonderful truths from God's Word. Everybody was reluctant to go back at the end of the day, ourselves included. We continued to pray that God's work would find fruitful ground in this most unlikely of places.

There was one Christian member of staff in this place. Her name was Maria and she was the widow of a pastor.

She was full of the Holy Spirit and a woman of great faith and she spoke to the women often about the Lord when she was working. Maria had a powerful, tuneful voice and loved singing Christian songs to them. She had worked there for thirty years and had seen some terrible things over the years. She could remember one week when six girls had died of hunger and cold. But she had prayed for God to have mercy on the women and girls who lived there. She was glad when we began visiting and together we prayed for the Lord's hand upon the place.

It began to be apparent that God was working in the lives of some of the women who lived there. We could see that some of them were drinking in spiritual truths and they had no difficulty believing what they heard. There were hearts prepared by the Holy Spirit to believe on the Lord Jesus Christ. They had so many questions! And the women had such a delight in hearing about God and, despite their context, possessed a joy in believing in this most wonderful Saviour who had brought such love to them. We saw lives being changed by the powerful working of God. It was clear to us that God had heard the cry of the women living there.

One day we arrived in one of the rooms where we knew that a number of the women had become Christians. Usually they would greet us with noise and great enthusiasm, but that morning was different. As we entered, one of the women, Anişoara, put her finger to her mouth and hushed us into silence. We were at a loss to understand this strange reception until we realised that the radio was on and they were all listening intently to somebody preaching. Once the sermon ended, they were happy to give us their customary attention.

On another occasion, we sat on their beds listening to a group of them singing a Christian song they had learnt. There are some beautiful Moldovan hymns, and this one spoke of heaven and the desire of the child of God to be there. As I listened, I thought again that there was no place I would rather be on this earth than in this poor place hearing such singing, It was as if we had entered an ante-room of heaven and we knew glory filling our souls.

From the beginning of the work, we felt ourselves to be passive observers of a mighty work of God. We were a tiny group of women with no influence and few resources. But we found ourselves in the presence of the most amazing God—One who works and no man can stay His hand and who flies on the wings of the wind. We worshipped and feared the high and lofty One who inhabits eternity and for whom nothing shall be impossible. We were awed by His determination to save.

I recalled one of our own hymns which says:

> *But lo! There breaks a yet more glorious day;*
> *The saints triumphant rise in bright array;*
> *The King of glory passes on his way.*
> *Hallelujah! Hallelujah!*

> *From earth's wide bounds, from ocean's farthest coast*
> *Through gates of pearl streams in the countless host,*
> *Singing to Father, Son and Holy Ghost.*
> *Hallelujah! Hallelujah!*

And I knew, with great assurance, that there would be saints from this place, who would rise in bright array on that day of days and see the King of glory. I knew, too, that there would be women from this institution, who would be amongst the countless host which will one day stream through those gates of pearl.

It caused me to reflect again on the character of God. Here was a God who had not forgotten a group of women, whom everybody else had forgotten. The death of His Son on Calvary for sinners, was efficacious here also. The One who had come to seek and save that which was lost had visited this shut-off place in kindness and grace and power, and women had seen something of His beauty. They had heard His voice calling "Follow me" and had eagerly run after Him. With ready willingness and with much joy they had found Him who truly loved them. Women experienced forgiveness for their sins and discovered a balm in Gilead for lives that had known so much suffering. What a Saviour!

They began to tell others about him. Anişoara was one of the first to be converted. She became an avid listener to the Christian radio broadcasts. Unable to read, these became her spiritual food. She learnt many Scripture verses by heart from the radio and the words of very many Christian hymns and songs. Anişoara noticed that there was a young woman, Diana, who used a wheelchair, who was having difficulty managing. She could not get to the table in time before the food had gone and would sit for long hours disconsolately on her own. Anişoara began to help Diana get to the table in time for meals and befriended her. This made the most enormous difference to Diana's days. Soon, Diana was listening to radio broadcasts at Anişoara's invitation, and was converted herself. They befriended another woman, Aliona, who was subsequently converted. And so it went on.

Before long it was obvious that there were a group of women who loved the Lord and were speaking about Him to anyone who would listen. They longed to be able to go to church and a number of them were asking about being baptised. These things were impossible for them to contemplate. Their lives were prescribed within the very narrow confines of a closed institution. The expectation was that when they reached a certain age, or the building became too full, that they would be moved to another closed institution for adults, where they would spend the rest of their lives.

Contemplating these things we began to dream of other possibilities for them. But wherever we looked, or whatever schemes we imagined, the realities were hard to escape. The women were in state care and we had no authority at all with regard to them. They had not been out for years and perhaps had never experienced a "normal" life in society. However could they cope on the outside? We had no resources. Although de-institutionalisation was developing quickly in countries like Romania, it had hardly started in Moldova and, because Moldova was not part of the European Union, there was not the same impetus for change. Everybody seemed to think that there was no better alternative. There was no precedent for setting up a home in the community for women with disabilities who had spent years in state "care". It had never been tried in Moldova. We were so few to contemplate undertaking such an enormous project. And even if we could start it, how could we keep it going? If it failed, that would be the death-knell to any future intervention on our part.

The potential difficulties did not stop here. Attitudes

towards people with disabilities were often harsh, even amongst Christians, and there was a general sense that the world was better without them. Mostly they spent their lives shut away either in institutions or at home with relatives, but mixing little outside of their families. Sometimes Christians and others thought that having a person with a disability in your family meant that you were cursed by God and this was an expression of His displeasure. They and their families were often not welcome in churches. There was no disabled access anywhere, including in churches. Everybody was so busy, genuinely trying to make ends meet, that they had no time or energy to give thought to those outside of their own extended family group.

How could anybody possibly begin to think about changing or challenging such a formidable array of obstacles? We were about to see "the exceeding greatness of His power toward us who believe" (Ephesians 1:19).

8

Anea and Liliana

... the work of faith with power
(2 Thessalonians 1:11)

I have already mentioned Anea, who was our driver on these excursions. She is now in her early fifties and was brought up in a village near the border with Romania. The river Prut separates the two countries and Romania is clearly visible across the river. Like so many Moldovan villages it does not have proper roads and in the autumn and winter negotiating its muddy tracks is quite a feat. Geese and ducks waddle nonchalantly along, in proud possession of its by-ways. In spring apple and cherry trees are full of beautiful blossom and in summer residents will paint their fences and houses bright blue or green.

There are a number of Christians in this place and

nowadays they have a large and beautiful church building in a prominent place at one end of the long sprawling village and another at the opposite end. One of the churches has written in large letters over the door, "Surely I am coming quickly" (Revelation 22:20). There is a flourishing work of God in the village and there is much freedom to reach men and women and boys and girls with the compelling message of God's love to us in Christ Jesus. Things used to be very different when Anea was a child.

Often, during winter evenings, Anea and I would sit chatting in her little flat, as she talked about her childhood. One of her earliest memories was of being woken up as a little child when the secret police arrived to search for Bibles which would have been brought by night for safe keeping in their house until they were distributed later in the city. It was a risky venture in human terms. Those found with stocks of Bibles in their possession faced interrogation and imprisonment. Anea did not have a Bible of her own until 1988; she was overjoyed to receive it, never expecting to have one. Hymn books and Bibles were hand-written in those days and if they were found they were burnt. Christians memorised very large portions of the Scripture and many hymns. I have often seen such hand-written books still being used by older believers today.

Anea's parents were both Christians and had both been widowed previously. Her mother, Vera, had been an Orthodox believer and used to attend Orthodox services regularly. She was married to a young man who was conscripted by the Russians to fight against the Germans, and was left caring for young twins. As the Germans passed through their village on their way to Moscow, which of course they never reached, they destroyed much in their path. Their house was almost totally razed by an exploding bomb. On the last day of the war in Germany Vera's husband at that time was killed in the battle for Berlin. It was a time of most grievous stress and suffering for her. Typhus swept through the village subsequently and both her children died as a result of the epidemic. In her complete desperation Vera had no idea where to turn for help. The services in the Orthodox church brought her little comfort. She had heard of a meeting of Baptists in a nearby village and decided that she would go there to see if there was anything there that could satisfy her soul and help her in her desolation. The Word she heard preached there thrilled her to the depths of her being. She cried out after the living God and on that very first visit she repented and believed. Vera found Him to be a very present help in trouble. A woman of very great faith, she was known as such in the whole village. Anea's home often became a refuge overnight for women who had been beaten by their drunken husbands, and her mother offered great kindness to such women and spoke to them of the Saviour.

Anea's father was very deaf and was unable to read and so her mother used to read the Scriptures to the family every day. When her father prayed, he prayed so loudly that all the neighbours could hear him as they passed the home. Although forbidden by the authorities, the "church" would meet in their house for prayer every week. The children of the family were known in the village as the offspring of the despised Baptists. At school Anea refused to wear the obligatory red scarf of the Pioneers, which signified allegiance to Lenin and the Communist Party. This was her own decision—her parents did not make the decision for her. In her young heart, whilst still not knowing for herself her parents' God, she began to count the cost of following their Saviour. And her heart longed to know this Saviour for herself.

Anea and her twin sister Dora and their brothers would often arrive at school to find that the teacher had drawn a picture of them on the blackboard, which made the other children laugh. The family were depicted as angels flying up to heaven with funny wings and halos. The teacher encouraged the other pupils to make fun of them. Little wonder the girls went to school with heavy feet. They were used to being pushed to the back of queues repeatedly in shops in the village and to being spat upon in the streets, but humiliation at school was another thing.

One day the headmistress came into the classroom with their teacher. This was unusual. Everybody feared the head teacher. She asked Anea to stand up and turn to a certain page in her reading book and read it out aloud to the class. Anea got to her feet trembling and hurriedly tried to find the page in question. It was not there. At the time she was eight years old, but she knew immediately that the teacher had torn the page out of her book. The same thing happened to her sister not many minutes later. The head teacher flew into a great rage and hauled the two children out to the front of the class and beat them mercilessly, until they could hardly stand. Returning home that day they told their mother they never wanted to go to school again. Their mother embraced them warmly and talked to them of One who knew everything His children suffered and of a love that understood the pain of nails in hands and feet and the deep humiliation of wearing a purple robe and a crown of thorns.

The next morning she put some fresh eggs in a basket for the children to take to school for the teacher and spoke to them of a love that is able to forgive even enemies.

Winters in the village were long and hard. The snow would be metres deep in the yard, but the cow still needed to be fed and the geese and hens attended to. Having a cow meant that they had milk and cheese, and on special occasions the children would receive the most splendid meal of mamaliga (a type of polenta) and warm milk. Children worked hard too, helping with the poultry and animals, working on the land and helping with chores in the home. There was little time for themselves.

Anea realised from an early age that her parents would fast and pray for two days each week. On one of these days they would pray especially for Christian pastors and Christian workers who were in prison and for their families. Her father visited the family members that remained when such men were taken off to prison or to camps in the Gulag, and regularly gave them money from their meagre income to help them. Those pastors hardly ever returned. The family used to receive information in secret each week on a news sheet about Christians in prison, including news about those who ran secret printing presses.

Anea longed to know her parents' God. She knew He was real, but she also knew from her mother's teaching that there was nothing automatic about her being a Christian just because she belonged to Christian parents, however godly and committed they were. She understood well that there needed to be a profound change in her own life, that she needed to repent personally and be born again of the Spirit of God. And she had learnt that in Soviet Moldavia there was a price to pay for choosing to follow this Man of Nazareth.

On Sundays Anea walked about ten kilometres each way to and from an unregistered church in another village which was brave enough to allow young people to attend, even though this was illegal and could lead to the pastor's arrest. She did not follow the normal roads, as it must not be suspected that she was going to church, but she would go by a back route, over fields and hills in all weathers, so that no one would see her. How she loved those services! They drew her to this glorious Redeemer who had shed His blood for her sins and she trusted Him with all her young heart. She was determined to be baptised and persuaded the pastor to baptise her at the age of fifteen. At the time, it was illegal for anyone under the age of eighteen to be baptised. Anea was baptised in a lake before dawn at a secret service soon afterwards.

There were days when, very early in the morning, a Communist official would knock on everybody's gate in the village and order people out, to make up the work forces. Anea would work out in the fields all day, sometimes in scorching heat, picking maize or sunflowers. Often they went without food or water all day. They would arrive home very late in a truck, exhausted. Late in the evenings Anea's mother would listen to the radio, which had been hidden away during the daytime. She would tune in to Radio Free Europe or other forbidden channels and listen for hours to wonderful preaching from men like Earl Poysti or Iosif Ton. These messages were nourishment to her soul. She told her children that a time was coming when everything would change—communism would end and they would be able to meet visitors from other countries. Anea remembered these things.

At the age of about fourteen it was customary for pupils at school to be summoned to join the Komsomol, the young people's branch of the Communist Party. Not to do so was to incur not only the wrath of the authorities but the scorn of fellow pupils. A spring day arrived when a bus came to collect all those excited pupils from Anea's class to an official ceremony and celebration initiating them all to the Komsomol. Anea and Dora decided they did not want to go and they stayed at home that day. Later all the young people returned to the village, full of pride at their new Komsomol status and Lenin insignia newly received. They scoffed at Anea and Dora and shouted at them that they would spend their lives working in the fields and would never find a good job because they had not joined the Party. It made no difference to the sisters; they did not regret not going despite the taunts they received.

Moldova is but a short distance from Chernobyl. At the time of the great explosion Anea was already living in Chișinău. They heard over the radio, three days after the explosion, that something had happened in a nuclear power station in the Ukraine. They were told to stay indoors and shut their windows. It was, of course, already too late. Her parents were still living in their village. The day after the disaster at Chernobyl their cow died, quite inexplicably as it seemed at the time; there had been nothing wrong with it the day before. A few months later, Anea's mother was diagnosed with stomach cancer. Very many adults and children were diagnosed with cancer and leukaemia at about the same time and very many children with disabilities were born.

By the time Vera's condition was diagnosed, the disease had already spread rapidly. A Jewish doctor kindly took Anea and Dora aside in the hospital and told them that it was too late for effective intervention. He said that even if other doctors told them the condition was curable, as indeed they had, in order to extract financial gain from them, this was not the truth. Vera went home to the village and her husband and sons and daughters cared for her. Many people came to see her—she was greatly loved by many—and she spoke to them all of a sure and certain hope in Jesus Christ and of heaven. The elders of the churches offered to pray with her for her healing but Vera declined their kind offer, knowing that this was not God's will for her. She used to say often to Anea, "Vreau acasa"—"I want to go home."

One night Vera had a vision and told her family of this. She told them that an angel had appeared to her and had told her that she would die in 120 days' time and that her funeral would be the occasion for a great evangelistic event, at which many people would be converted. And so it happened. Anea and her sister were in the garden of their parents' house late one afternoon in 1989 and heard their mother calling urgently to them. She cried out, "He has come for me! Oh! can you see him? My Saviour has come for me!" And she died that evening. It was 120 days after the vision.

In those days evangelism was not allowed, but Christians would use occasions like funerals to preach evangelistic messages. However all that was permitted was for a brother to speak in the house before the coffin left and for another brother to preach at the graveside. A very great crowd of people attended the funeral procession. People had come from many neighbouring villages, as well as from the city, and the streets were teeming with a multitude of people. It is usual in Moldova for the open coffin to be carried, usually a long distance, to the place of burial. As the coffin was carried and the crowd followed, at frequent intervals the procession would stop and a pastor or a Christian brother would preach to those assembled, calling people to repentance and faith in the Lord Jesus. This was the first time that people could remember that the Gospel had been preached so frequently during a funeral procession. There were many rumours circulating at the time about the possible fall of communism and the brothers were very bold in taking encouragement from this possibility. It became an evangelistic outreach the like of which was unknown in living memory. Many were converted on that day, including a number of Anea's relatives who had thus far shown no interest in the Gospel. One of her mother's sisters was too ill to attend. At home on her own that day she was thoroughly convicted of her need for forgiveness and was saved.

Like so many others Anea was not allowed access to any kind of higher education because of her Christian faith, but in her late teens, and on the advice of her mother, she went to live in Chișinău. She was given a job in a big factory and lived in a room in a hostel, which she shared with three other women. Working days were long, often from seven in the morning to seven at night, and there was voluntary work in honour of Lenin which used up precious Saturdays far too frequently. Dora worked in the same factory. They noticed a young woman working alongside them, whose behaviour marked her out from the others. Anea said to Dora, "She has something of Christ about her." The woman in question was Tanea, who was to become a close supporter of the work in Moldova.

All the factory staff were obliged to attend the communist events in the factory from time to time. Neither Anea, nor Dora, nor Tanea ever joined the Communist Party, which would have been a sure route to rapid job progress. It was customary, when employees became members of the Communist Party, for there to be a special celebration which all the factory workers were required to attend. The person joining the Party was always asked, in very serious tones, why they wanted to join the Party, and the expectation was that the new member would give a short prepared speech singing the praises of the Party. On one particular occasion the new recruit was a woman who, in answer to the question, and completely overwhelmed by the auspicious nature of the event, simply replied in Russian, "I love it!" Nobody could prevent the assembled throng from disintegrating into howls of laughter! The Party lost face just a little that day.

Anea, Dora and Tanea were regularly called in for questioning about their faith and religious activities by the authorities. Everybody knew that they were Christians. For one thing, they were the only ones who did not steal from the factory. It was common for this kind of theft to go on in state enterprises, employees justifying it to themselves as a means of supplementing their low wages. But these women never stole. They had just about enough to live on, but no more than the absolute necessities. They had been told repeatedly that Moldova was one of the richest countries in Europe and that people in Western countries were suffering great unemployment and acute poverty. It was virtually impossible to meet with those from Western countries and to have a discussion with them, so many believed this to be the truth. Anea, however, was not convinced: her mother had heard different things on the radio.

There are not many spare minutes in Anea's day. She worked at the same factory for over thirty years until 2012, when she felt the call of God to leave and devote all her time to Christian work. She is a woman of the most incredible energy and faith, with a heart that praises God in whatever situation she finds herself. One of the enduring impressions is of Anea praying before a meal, when I have known that the day has been hard for her and one might think there was little to rejoice about. Without fail, she will praise God with all her heart for the wonderful day He has given her, for the grace He has provided for her and for His love in Christ Jesus. The joy of the Lord has become her strength, and there is an abundance in that joy and a heart that has learnt to be thankful, which can be seen.

Anea loves the saints and delights to serve God's people in whatever way she can. Importantly, this sometimes takes the form of driving folk around. Having a car now and being a fearless driver, she will often be found taking friends where they need to go in the Lord's work. Her walk with the Lord is close and trusting and she has seen remarkable answers to prayers many times. Anea loves to talk about her Saviour and He is brought into her conversation in the most natural of ways all the time. At our first meeting, we had no way of knowing how the Lord would open up a work for us together. Anea was still feeling the loss of her mother keenly. She was working full-time, looking after her adopted daughter, Galina, and busy in the church. But she wanted to do more for the Lord. When she moved to Chişinău, her mother had said to her that the Lord had prepared a great work for her there. With time Anea had forgotten those words. But she had cause to remember them later.

When we are asked to speak about our work in different churches in Moldova, Anea will recall how she spent her life simply working in a factory. She will share how she had not the slightest idea about places where people with problems or with disabilities lived, isolated from the world and sometimes in very poor conditions. This all changed when she made her first visit with us to that institution on the hill. She could not believe what her eyes saw, and this in a place not very far from her home village that she had passed times beyond number. After seeing these things she found it difficult to eat or to sleep for a week. She could not get the people out of her mind or heart. Fervent prayer for them filled her thoughts and she became determined, by God's grace, to try to do something to help. Anea has become one of the main supports for our work and was to play a vital role in God's plan.

Liliana, who now heads up the work, almost died a few months after she was born. She became very seriously ill and was unconscious for some days. She had developed meningitis and her temperature was very high indeed. Her mother was advised to plunge her into a bath of frozen water to lower her temperature! The doctor told her parents that she would not live, and relatives prepared a tiny coffin for her. But live she did, although she lost her hearing completely in her right ear.

Liliana became acquainted with the Gospel originally as a

little child, from Anea's mother, Vera, who used to look after her whilst both her parents were working. Very soon Vera knew that the Lord had His hand upon Liliana and that she would be His. Nobody in Liliana's close family was converted at that time, and Liliana loved being with Vera, especially when Christians would meet secretly to pray in that house. She learnt their hymns from an early age and would sit on the wall of her own house singing them to herself. Soon a pastor and his family moved next door to her and she wanted so much to go to church with them, but there was never room in the car and children were not encouraged to go to church regularly. The Lord had put a deep thirst after Himself in Liliana's heart, which nothing else could satisfy.

One day at school a teacher questioned Liliana about her faith and her Christian friends. "Do you know how to pray?" the teacher asked. "Of course," Liliana guilelessly replied, and she began to recite the Lord's Prayer. "And where did you learn that?" she was asked. She told the teacher about Vera and the people who prayed in her house. "And do you know any of their songs and hymns?" Liliana treated the teacher to a rendering of one of the hymns she had learnt. "And where are these hymns written down?" Immediately Liliana replied that they were all written down in a hymn book which was in her sister's bag! The bag in question was found and the hand-written hymn book removed. That night there was a knock on the gate of their family home. Her mother went to see who the caller was. Liliana's teacher was at the gate in angry mood. She accused Liliana's mother of allowing her daughter to attend dangerous "Baptist" meetings and showed her the hymn book which had been taken. Liliana's mother was instructed to keep her daughter away from all such harmful gatherings in the future or she would lose her place in the school. To Liliana's consternation she was told to stay away from Vera's house. She never saw the hymn book again, but the Lord continued His powerful work in her heart and she came into a personal relationship with Him soon afterwards. At the age of seventeen she publicly repented in a church, but the Lord had worked a very long time before this in her heart and called her to Himself. She is now in her thirties, and has a spiritual maturity well beyond her years and a life that visibly communicates the love of Christ to those with whom she comes into contact. Quite simply, she lives for the Saviour and her life is an outpouring of love and service for Jesus Christ. She has learnt ready and willing obedience to His voice and to fear sinning against Him.

9

Tanea and the Family

By faith Abraham obeyed ... And he went out ...
(Hebrews 11:8)

Tanea is the kind of person you would not look at twice in a crowd. She has straight, unruly hair and a sallow complexion. Of average height, her clothes are neat but drab, her voice is quiet and her manner reserved. In her early fifties, she is unmarried and has worked all her life in the factory where Anea formerly worked. They are the best of friends. Tanea is a remarkable woman. She is full of the love of Christ and walks very closely with Him and is a woman of much prayer. Her life is a living sacrifice to the Saviour and heaven will reveal how much treasure she has laid up there.

There have been occasions when Tanea has recounted to me memories of her younger days when she had to walk very considerable distances to and from work—nearly twenty kilometres a day. She has told me that she would spend the whole journey in communion with the Saviour, in very precious fellowship with Him whom her soul loves. Her friends have related to me how she was picked out by the communists for very particular persecution, which she faced bravely and without any bitterness towards her enemies. There is a holiness to her daily walk which seemed to attract much opposition, despite her quiet, reserved nature.

Tanea lives on the sixth floor of a poor apartment block. There is no lift and it is a very long haul upstairs, particularly with a lot of shopping. The lights on the stairs are often not working and in the winter the uneven, concrete steps have to be carefully negotiated in the dark. The flat itself is small and a little damp. It is never very warm in winter, but in the summer it can be very hot. Nine people and a cockatoo have lived in this little flat. Tanea has been a foster carer to seven young people whom she has cared for for many years, together with Liliana who helps her in this task.

Converted as a young person during the burdensome days of communism, Tanea learnt at an early age to count the cost of following Christ. She became strong in faith and with a heart devoted to God. She was not unused to seeing the God of miracles at work. Whilst in her early twenties Tanea had a vision of the Lord Jesus Christ. She has never forgotten this. He said to her, "Feed my lambs". The full meaning of what she had seen only became clearer later.

A member of a Russian speaking church, Tanea went regularly to its services whenever she could. One Sunday there was an unusual announcement. Someone spoke at the end of the service about four children who had been

abandoned and were now in hospital. The person asked if
anybody in the congregation could find it in their heart to
help. Tanea describes how she felt compelled to go to the
front to ask about the children; she heard the Lord Himself
calling her to do this. Enquiring about their whereabouts,
she went to visit them.

The oldest girl was twelve years old and the youngest, the
only boy, was six. Tanea's first sight of the children scared
her. Their heads were shaved and they were shut up in a
dilapidated ward. The children were very thin and their
behaviour was wild and animal-like. But she visited them
often and prayed. She determined that she would take on
the responsibility for these children and was certain that
this was what the Lord was asking her to do. Her income
was tiny and the challenge of caring for such children
on a permanent basis was enormous. They were all very
disturbed by what was evidently a very traumatic past.
One of the girls had a moderate learning disability and
another had frequent epileptic seizures. They all looked
considerably younger than their chronological ages. How
could a young, single woman with no resources to speak of
begin to contemplate taking on such a role?

It was enough for Tanea that she had heard God's call. She
did not hesitate to do as He asked her. The children visited
her a few times and soon she obtained all the necessary
permissions and they came to live with her. She asked
Liliana if she would be willing to help her. At the time Liliana
was eighteen years old and a student at the university. It was
a massive undertaking for such a young woman but Liliana
sought the Lord about this and agreed to help. She moved in
with Tanea and the children.

Soon after the children moved in one of their relatives, an uncle, came to visit. Immediately the children knew who had arrived they started trembling and rushed to hide anywhere they could in the flat. The oldest girl started screaming. The visit was a short one and nobody from their family had any further contact with them. Little by little the story of the children's lives started to become clearer. Tanea and Liliana learnt that neighbours had called in the police after they had heard one of the children having a terrible beating. Even the police were horrified by what they discovered. One of the girls was nine and was still unable to walk. All the children had bloated stomachs because of starvation. They had suffered the most dreadful abuse of every kind. The oldest girl had been sent to buy alcohol regularly for her drunken relatives. The children were taken to hospital and life in long term institutions was what was in view for all of them.

The young boy was terrified of having a bath and nobody understood why until they realised that when he had cried previously he had been punished by having his head held under cold water until he was on the point of drowning. Young as he was, and being the only boy in the family, he had felt responsible for making sure that his sisters were all right and was constantly trying to ensure they were taken care of. It took a long time for him to realise that Tanea and Liliana were now able to share this responsibility with him. All the children were literally starving. Tanea and Anea still remember one of the first meals when the children demolished a huge casserole of food in lightning time, tearing the meat apart with their hands and gorging it as quickly as they could until there was nothing left. Everything disappeared!

Few people would have considered taking on such a responsibility. Although Tanea received a small allowance to care for the children it was by no means adequate to sustain them. Here were a group of very disturbed children, at least two of whom would probably require life-time support. Even her own pastor advised her against it initially; he was influenced by the view that children with disabilities were of no real value and were better cared for in appropriate institutions. But Tanea had received a commission from the Lord and it was His well- known voice that she chose to obey.

In 2000 another three children joined the household—a six year old boy and twins aged eight. The three were all from the same family and had been abandoned by parents and relatives and were living in a children's institution. The small flat became even more crowded and Tanea and Liliana looked even more to the Lord to supply all that was needed for this growing family. As with any family they have shared great trials and joys but they have never lacked sufficient for their daily needs. In the most amazing way the Lord has provided for them.

The children learnt from an early age to seek this God of wonders. Kneeling together each evening, they learnt to call upon the One who opens His hand and satisfies the needs of every living thing and again and again they proved that He answers prayer. And one by one some of them came to know Him for themselves, whom to know is life eternal.

My mind is full of so many warm memories of times spent with this family in their top-floor flat. A great crowd will squeeze into their biggest room and gather round a large table which will be adorned with a pristinely white tablecloth upon which wonderful dishes will appear in rapid succession for the honoured visitors. Both the young men and women enjoy cooking and they will have spent much of the day shopping and preparing great delicacies. The assembled gathering will sit chatting for hours and Tanea will ask quiet, searching questions about what the Lord is teaching us and how He is working. She will communicate her deep thankfulness for the prayers of the saints for herself and the children. Both Tanea and Liliana will talk about His care for them. The Lord will be the centre of the conversation.

One day I recorded Tanea's testimony:

"I went to a small village school and left when I was fifteen years old. We were living in a village and when it rained the streets were just mud. But we loved it there—the woods were near; in the summer it was quiet and the air was fresh. It was an unforgettable time.

I had believed in God since I was a very small child. I never doubted that He existed. Nobody else around me believed in Him. At school nobody told us about God—to the contrary in fact. We had a lot of lessons telling us there was no God. In my school report when I left they wrote, "She does not belong to the Komsomolists." It was a struggle to get any further education because of this.

I was eighteen when I was converted and nineteen when I was baptised. All my life I had loved to be with Christian people and I loved to attend church. There was a Pentecostal church in our village which I used to attend but when I came to the city a sister took me to her church. It was a Baptist church and it was the only church that was open in the city at that time. There were preachers then in Russian and Romanian.

The church has changed since then although it's essentially the same. They have always preached about the need for repentance and faith. They have had some great preachers there and I've heard many profound messages which have affected me. The messages were always simple but you knew that the Holy Spirit had inspired them. The singing was inspired also.

When I repented I so longed to be rid of my sin. I so wanted to be holy and to be without sin. I tried to do everything to get rid of my sin until I finally realised that it was all in vain and that I needed to repent. When I repented I knew that He had died for me and that He had taken away all my sin. I told everybody what had happened to me. I can remember telling a lie once when I was ten years old and being so convicted about it afterwards. I remember telling God that I was very sorry for telling a lie and I felt even then that He had forgiven me. I did not understand then that Jesus had died for me. I knew that God was good and that if I prayed to Him, He would forgive me.

After school I started to work in a factory. They found out that I was a Christian there and they asked for my dismissal from the factory. A friend of mine who was Pentecostal was thrown out of the factory at the same time. We had enemies there. I managed to get another job in a bread factory. I worked there for two years and then I went to work in a factory in Moscow for a year. There was a very big Baptist church in Moscow which I used to attend. I loved going to that church but I got very homesick. That's why I left Moscow. There would have been much better material opportunities in Moscow. For example, if you worked for three years in the construction industry you qualified for an apartment. But I was so homesick these possibilities did not tempt me.

I got a job back in Chișinău. After I was converted I had very close fellowship with God. I experienced indescribable joy during those first years. When I woke up in the mornings I was full of joy in the Lord. Some friends of ours were leaving to go to America and I went to see them the evening before they left. One of them asked me, "How is it that you never seem to have any problems?" He thought that was really the case. I knew that I had a wonderful eternal future waiting for me. I was never well off but I knew that I had all that I needed. I used to sing, "God is with us" day and night. I was full of songs of praise to Him.

Now our parents need our help and problems come with children. I never wanted to be away from fellowship with God.

I was working two shifts so I was not able to join the prayer circle. Prayer isn't something very formal for me. I talk to Him as I'm walking along the road, or often in the night I will wake up and pray. At one time I used to have a very long walk to work and I spent all the time praying as I walked. I longed for fellowship with God. I can remember a preacher once told us that he learned to pray on the doorstep of his house as his wife would not allow him to pray at home. After a long time his wife repented as well. We used to have some wonderful preachers in those days."

And so the Lord prepared, equipped and gathered together a small group of totally insignificant women who would draw no particular attention or interest on the part of this world. He trained them, often in a school of suffering and complete dependence on Him for every single need. They followed hard after Him and learnt to trust Him in every circumstance of life. He was absolutely to be trusted in good and ill. Prayer became their life breath and they entered into close communion with their Redeemer. They walked with Him as Enoch of old. Their experience had taught them that, "with God nothing will be impossible" (Luke 1:37). They looked to a great God of wonders and believed His promises. Not trusting an iota in their human wisdom or resources and realising that their treasure was contained in very earthen vessels, when the Lord began to work they made it clear to all that it was the excellency of His power at work and no mere human effort. They were vessels "meet for the Master's use."

10

The First House—Casa Bucuriei

*Did I not say to you that if you would believe
you would see the glory of God?*
(John 11:40)

A warm summer's afternoon in Cardiff found me among a group of people enjoying afternoon tea in the garden of some friends who had kindly opened their home for us. There were umbrellas for the shade and delicious scones decked the tables. It had been planned that I should speak about the work in Moldova and our desire to start a house for some of the women from the institution we had been visiting. The gathering was not a large one, but those present showed a genuine interest in the work and asked a number of questions afterwards. It was not long after that memorable afternoon that I returned to Moldova. This was the only meeting at which I spoke of the house at that time.

I have never been very good at what the professionals call "profile raising" or "networking". There has always been a natural reluctance to draw attention to work in which I am involved, and fund-raising in a Christian context has never sat happily with me. Strongly influenced by what I had read of Hudson Taylor and the China Inland Mission, I was inwardly persuaded to learn to "move man through God by prayer alone." If the God in whom I trusted was the God who created the heavens and the earth by the work of His power I could not see that He would have the slightest difficulty supplying the resources we needed to purchase a house. It did not depend on any feeble attempts on my part to ask people to supply our needs. The Lord could so work to make this possible. Our part was to pray that He would do this.

The meeting in the garden took place in July 2006. In October that year, I was in Moldova and one day I received a text message from a close friend at home: "All monies needed to buy house have been found!" I dashed into the next room to share the news with Anea and Liliana and we fell on our faces to praise God with very full hearts. We cried with joy at the news we had received. What a great God!

A serious quest began to find a suitable house or land. Newspaper adverts were read and placed, friends were telephoned to see if anyone knew of a suitable property and fervent prayer went up to heaven for direction to the place of the Lord's own choosing. Most of the work in actually viewing properties rested with Liliana and Anea. The search was by no means an easy one, and we laughed together many times as they regaled me with tales of houses they had viewed that nobody in their right minds would consider purchasing. There was the house that looked as though it were ready to collapse on its poor occupants, or the one that had a view of the sky through the roof, not to mention the one to which access was so formidable as to present an enormous challenge to the most able-bodied. The months went on and they continued the search as the weather grew hot and humid. They developed a detailed knowledge of all the surrounding villages and of all the available properties on the market. But they drew a blank. It seemed that there was absolutely nothing suitable for our needs.

Both of them were exhausted with the search. They had run out of ideas about where to look further. Since the beginning of the work we had always held Fridays as a day of prayer and fasting for the work. It was a Friday evening and Anea was praying that the Lord would open a door. Then she remembered Sister Liudmila in the village of Truşeni, just outside Chişinău. Yes, she did know of somewhere. One of the sisters in her church had told her of a property next door to her which was for sale. She was praying for Christian neighbours and she had told Sister Liudmila about this.

Liliana and Anea went over to see the house immediately. It was just what they were looking for! It was partially built, on a largish piece of land just a short walk away from a very good evangelical church. The property, although unfinished, was well built and the couple who were selling it were willing to include all the building materials they had purchased in the price. There was space sufficient for a number or rooms to be added to the building and still leave a good piece of ground at the back for growing vegetables and keeping animals and poultry. Some friends went to examine the property to check its worthiness to purchase and advised us that it was a very good buy indeed. Liliana explained that we would like to buy the property and the current owners accepted our offer, providing the purchase could be made within a designated period of time.

At the time I was in the UK and I rapidly purchased a plane ticket to Moldova in order to bring the sum needed for the purchase. The responsibility weighed heavily on me. Bank transfers could not be relied on, as banks frequently failed or money "disappeared" in transit. The only way to be sure of getting the money there on time was to take it. I was comforted by Psalm 121: "He who keeps you will not slumber ... The Lord shall preserve you from all evil ... The Lord shall preserve your going out and your coming in" (Psalm 121: 3, 7, 8). And I was challenged by another verse that often spoke to me, "Do not be unbelieving, but believing" (John 20:27).

In terms of any possible trust in human strength and wisdom for the journey ahead, the week preceding my departure was hardly propitious. I had lost my purse containing all my cards and cash whilst out cycling. Amazingly, it was handed in to the police station and I recovered everything. Another day that same week I returned from the dentist to discover that I had absent-mindedly left on the cooker something which was about to catch fire. Due to catch a coach to the airport in the middle of the night, I arrived there with a friend much too early as I had not checked the time on the ticket.

To cap it all, arriving at the airport very early in the morning I began searching for my passport and discovered, to my absolute horror, that I could not find it! What was even worse was that I had no memory of having packed it. To have been so irresponsible, when so many people had given so much to the house, and I could not even be relied on to pack my passport! I can remember sitting on the floor of the airport, searching through all my belongings, frantically trying to find the missing passport, and shaking with the emotion of it all. And suddenly, I found the passport—in a pocket in my hand luggage I did not even know existed. With what thankfulness I praised the Lord.

Budapest was reached without further problems. The flight to Moldova from Hungary, took off on time. There were about fifty of us crushed into the usual small propeller plane. The weather was hot—it was early June. It was not long before the journey became perilous in the extreme. In all the travelling I had done over the years, to and from Moldova, this was the journey that could not be forgotten! It was as if we had boarded an aerial roller-coaster. We would mount to the top of an invisible tsunami wave in the sky, and then, as quickly, plunge to the depths in a fall that felt as though it could not possibly be halted. This continued for most of the journey. The warning lights came on quickly and the elderly Moldovan gentleman sitting next to me grabbed my arm in fright. Behind us there was trouble brewing. Whereas I suspect the British may be capable of perhaps sitting, stiff upper-lipped, and quietly dying in this kind of crisis, Moldovans are made of different stuff. Of Latin, as well as Slavic extraction, despite being ordered over the intercom to remain in their seats a large number of people started to get out of their seats in panic and were trying to walk around the plane. Not surprisingly, they were being thrown about by the turbulence of the plane and were putting themselves in even greater danger. It was very noisy; the cabin crew were nowhere to be seen, but screamed orders at the passengers to sit down. The passengers in turn were shouting at each other in their fear. It was a scene of utter chaos.

With a sense of enormous relief we eventually landed safely in Chişinău and found ourselves being disgorged from the aircraft in an emotionally weakened state. The force of hot air met us as we climbed down the plane steps. I was conscious that the real challenges were but beginning. From the start I had settled in my mind that I did not want to be involved in anything illegal in terms of taking money into the country. Thus I had resolved to declare the amount I was carrying to the customs officer. I also had letters from my home church explaining that the money had been given for bona fide purposes. However, I was not naive about the reputation of customs officials and was very aware that the Lord needed to perform a great miracle to get the money through untouched. As I approached the first officials my prayer was that God would make seeing eyes blind, and hearing ears deaf. Many times, in years gone by, I had seen the Lord work miracles at impossible checkpoints in Eastern Europe, when Christian literature was being transported, and I had much experience of this prayer being answered. Gathering my luggage I walked towards a female customs officer. I said that I wanted to declare money I was bringing into the country, in both pounds and euros. At this stage I could see Liliana and Anea waving to me with great enthusiasm beyond the customs point. The customs officer asked me how many pounds I had with me. I answered that I had £500. She then pointed towards the exit and told me, using the strong Romanian imperative form, to go. I went! Although I had said that I had both pounds and euros, it was as if she had not heard the word "euros" and all the money for the house was in euros. God had made hearing ears deaf again. With what joy and thankfulness to God, we all embraced on the other side of the barrier! I texted friends at home to say, "The vehicle called Little Faith, has arrived safely in one piece after some adventures. To God be the glory!"

It was not long after I arrived that I was whisked off for a first viewing of the new house. Truşeni is known as the "village of cherries" and as we entered it there was row after row of cherry trees which had recently fruited on either side of the road. There was a small, roughly laid-out square in the centre of the village, with the Casa de Cultura (the former Communist House of Culture), and a small one-storey town hall sporting a bright Moldovan flag outside. Up the hill we went towards a large Orthodox church on which a new tower was being constructed, passing a large number of dwellings behind traditional Moldovan fences and gates.

Though still unfinished, it was obvious at once that our new house was an excellent choice. There was an old, ruined house in the grounds, which was later to be demolished, surrounded by cherry and pear trees. A much-needed well was located in the garden and the nearest village well was but a short walk down the street. We talked excitedly of a day when chickens and geese would be kept and when land behind the house would be planted up with fruitful crops. There was a big, cold cellar under the house and we imagined how it would look when it would be stocked with provisions for the winter. But there was still a long way to go. The inside of the house was but a shell, apart from one or two rooms, and a concrete-making basin occupied the first room. There was no furniture to speak of, only a bedroom with a mattress on the floor and a tiny gas stove on a rickety table. Only one room had any heating. It was clear that there was a great amount of work still to be tackled. But this was the house God had given us, of that there was not the slightest doubt, and how we praised Him.

For the first time I met some members of the family who lived next door—Sister Galina and her two sons, Nicu and Emanuel and daughter, Mariana. It was a thrilling meeting for us all. She was rejoicing in the way that the Lord had answered her prayer for Christian neighbours. None of us knew then quite how important this family would be in the future in God's amazing providence.

At the same time that the search for the house was under way there were a number of other complex obstacles that needed to be negotiated. Taking women with disabilities out of a long-stay institution, and giving them a permanent home in an ordinary community, was very new for Moldova. Although we were aware of one other successful house project in a village, which had been initiated by Christians, the people that it served did not have disabilities. Ours was pioneer ground, and permission was required at the highest Government levels to proceed with our plans. It was also essential for us to set up a Moldovan-registered non-governmental organisation as a legally-constituted entity.

Morning broke on the tenth of March 2006, bitterly cold with a blizzard of snow sweeping us along the street as we walked towards one of the Government buildings in the city. A crucial appointment with a Government minister, who had the authority to make a decision on our proposal to start the house, had been arranged. Without permission we would be unable to proceed. We arrived in good time in the front lobby of the offices in question. Before leaving home, we had prayed together and, very conscious of our own great weakness and inability, had cast ourselves completely on the Lord.

A fierce female official accosted us in the lobby. She was wearing a thick, winter coat and a large, fur hat. We explained that we had an appointment with the Minister, but she responded most aggressively, shouting at us that the Minister was not in the building that day, and had no appointments with anyone. She would not permit us to go up the stairs to his office. What were we to do? For many minutes, we stood in the freezing lobby, pondering our next course of action. The way to the Minister was barred, but we had no intention of leaving the building and abandoning such an important appointment. We silently prayed.

Suddenly, in through the front door, blown in seemingly by the blast of the blizzard, entered the Director of the institution where the women were living. After greeting us warmly, she stormed into the building, ignoring the female official, who rapidly stood aside when she saw the Director approaching. We were beckoned to follow her as she swept up a long flight of stairs in majestic fashion and we ran to keep up with her. Reaching the top of the stairs she marched along a narrow corridor and entered a room on the left. Greeting the Minister's secretary with the briefest of courtesies, she knocked on the door to the Minister's room and entered confidently, commanding us to enter also.

We could hardly believe it. In a few minutes we had been ushered into the very presence of the Minister himself! He asked us to sit down opposite him at a very long table. A large photo of the President of Moldova, Voronin, was staring down at us. Liliana began to present the house project proposal, both articulately and confidently. I glanced sideways at her during the presentation, thanking God for the gifts He had given to His servant for such a time as this. The Director spoke very warmly in our support. The Minister questioned us on a number of matters and within about half an hour, the whole meeting had ended. He gave us his permission to proceed with what he referred to as "this interesting little experiment."

It was in a daze of excitement and thankfulness that we walked out into the corridor. The Director hugged us and wished us well and left for another meeting on the same floor. We walked down the stairs, past the woman who had forbidden us access and out into the snow. As we walked along we sang "How great Thou art!" in Romanian and English and praised the God of heaven, who alone does wonders. It was less than a week before the women were to move into Casa Bucuriei (House of Joy) that we received the final, written, authorised government permission to move them. I have a photo of Liliana, smiling with delight and holding the said document.

We drew much encouragement from some verses in 2 Chronicles: "Do not be afraid or dismayed before the king of Assyria, nor before all the multitude that is with him; for there are more with us than with him. With him is an arm of flesh; but with us is the Lord our God, to help us and to fight our battles" (2 Chronicles 32:7–8). It was only the

Lord who gave us the strength to persevere when the odds looked impossibly against us. One incident stands out in my memory exactly one week before Casa Bucuriei was due to be opened. Time was very short and it was still far from ready. The six women who were to live in the house had been allowed to come from the institution for the day, to help prepare everything. At lunchtime we had our first meal together in the new house, in the basement. We ate standing up, as there were hardly any chairs yet, but it was a great feast of thanksgiving for all those present. Diana, one of the six women, could not stop smiling.

All the women worked so hard, but it seemed as soon as we tried to clean one room the men who were working on the house needed to do something in that room and the floor became dirty yet again. It was a chilly October day and in the afternoon I took some of the women out into the garden at the back. It was in desperate need of being at least dug over and the rubbish cleared before the opening. I could hardly cope at that stage with the state of things indoors and thought we might re charge our batteries in the open air. It was a dull, cloudy afternoon and a very cold wind was blowing through the village; winter was not far away, one felt. We started a bonfire to burn some of the rubbish and our clothes were, by this time, very dirty and smelling of smoke. What happened then is hard to describe. We knew that there were angels singing. In that most ordinary of scenes we knew that heaven was rejoicing. In the outward bleakness of that afternoon suddenly eternity broke into our little time and we knew that God was very near. I think I will never forget that day, or the days that followed. We had a sense of God rejoicing over the work of His hands, and heaven with Him, and we were awed by His presence and worshipped Him with full hearts.

And so, the God "who works all things according to the counsel of His will" (Ephesians 1:11) guided us with His eye and removed every obstacle out of our path, so that the house would become a reality. We watched His glorious ways.

11

Opening of Casa Bucuriei

He does according to His will in the army of heaven
and among the inhabitants of the earth
no one can restrain His hand
(Daniel 4:35)

I t was 3rd November 2006 and our visitors from my home church in Cardiff, including the pastor, had arrived for the opening of Casa Bucuriei. We were awake very early in the morning for this most important day, the day when the six women were due to move into their new home. Anea spoke to me as soon as I was up to say that they had received a phone call late at night from Maria, the Christian member of staff who worked at the institution. Maria had said that an aid worker from the West, who had a lot of influence with the Director, had stirred up a great commotion by saying that we were trying to change the women's religion. As a consequence the Director was re-thinking her position on the women's release. To fall at this very last hurdle was unthinkable. Everything was ready. Months of work and years of involvement had brought us to this point. The women were eagerly expecting to be released to their new home. The official house opening was scheduled for the following day. But, in ourselves, we were totally helpless in the face of such opposition. Although we had the papers in our hands, giving us ministerial authority for the women to be removed, the Director could still veto this. Anea called us all to prayer.

We all knelt around the room crying out to the Lord to help us. We had only Him on whom to call for aid. Many times in Moldova, the Lord brings us into a position where we have no human remedy to our situation at all and we are driven to turn to Him in sheer desperation. This was one such time, and we were heard, in the Lord's mercy. "Their prayer came up to His holy dwelling place, to heaven" (2 Chronicles 30:27).We drove the sixty or so kilometres to the institution and entered the Director's office. The Director was glowering as we came in and did not greet us with her usual customary warmth. There was no eye contact from her and she asked us in a curt manner to introduce ourselves. How fervently we were praying throughout these preliminaries and the discussion that followed! After some harsh comments and a blaze of fury about a missing document that we should have brought with us we were in a state of great alarm. I can remember, however, that Liliana and Anea remained calm. So often, I had seen them leaning upon the Lord in a time of crisis and enjoying communion with Him.

Unexpectedly, the Director began to cry. She said that she was going to miss the women terribly and would be visiting them regularly to ensure that everything was OK. At this our hearts soared. She reminded us severely, that she had the right to take them back at any time if she was not happy with the situation. Eventually she said the all-important word "bine", which meant that everything could go ahead and we knew that the women were free. We left the room with very great thanksgiving and rejoicing to break the final news to the women. They had been ready, packed and with their outdoor clothes on since early that morning and there was a momentous atmosphere throughout the whole institution. Everyone seemed to realise that an event of very great significance was taking place. The place was buzzing with excitement and rumour. Many of the women asked us if we could take them with us too and it was very hard to be unable to respond positively to all. They had realised that the talk of a house outside was in fact a reality and now many longed for such an opportunity. The Director had ordered one of her drivers to escort the women in a minibus from the institution. Despite the fact that the six women were ready to leave, the paperwork and organisational necessities for this most unusual of occurrences took a long time. At last everything was in order. A great crowd of women and staff had gathered to see the six women off and the Director made her way down to the minibus to make her final farewells. She was by this time, smiling, but tearful. As we left, crushed together in Anea's car, following the minibus, there was a huge crowd of women and staff waving. The gates opened for the first and last time for the women and they were released.

It is hard to describe the mood in Anea's car during that journey. A friend who was present said "We are looking at a miracle" and we all knew that was the case. We followed the minibus to Truşeni, occasionally losing sight of it and then overtaking to see the beaming smiles of the women. At one point we had to get out of the car as we drove across a field that could not be negotiated with all of us on board. And so we reached Casa Bucuriei. We were like those that dream.

The house was due to be formally opened the following day. We had delivered invitations to neighbours, friends, those from the institution and the local mayor, and the women from the church were to prepare food for everybody. Everything was ready except the house. Anyone who saw it the day before the opening would have been hard-pressed to believe that it could possibly be ready in a day's time. The outside driveway was not laid; there was builder's equipment everywhere; most of the rooms were not yet completely finished and chaos seemed to be reigning. None of this had a negative effect on the new occupants of the home. They found a corner for their meagre belongings and set to work immediately to help with the housework. We worked together for hours—there were beds to be assembled, curtains to be put up and rooms to be cleaned. In the evening we collapsed into chairs and saw that the house was beginning to look like a home. But nevertheless it was impossible to think that everything would be ready in time for the morning. We returned late at night to Chişinău and sank exhausted into slumber.

The opening day was a Saturday and, after rising early

and praying together, we set off, crushed together in the car, en route to Truşeni and the opening service, with great anticipation. As we arrived at Casa Bucuriei, we could not believe our eyes. The most incredible transformation had occurred since we had left a few hours earlier. The drive had been laid and looked most impressive; flower beds had been dug and even planted; balloons festooned the outside of the house; and a special red ribbon had been attached across the outside staircase. The inside of the house was immaculate, with not the slightest sign of builder's equipment or disorder. Liliana shared with us that the men had worked through most of the night, whilst she held a lamp to help them see what they were doing.

Our six friends were dressed in their best finery and beaming with pleasure. Crowds began arriving and it was not long before the outside courtyard was full and the service began. Pastor Wyn Hughes from Cardiff and the local mayor cut the ribbon and we all entered the house to beautiful music, noisy conversation and untold rejoicing. It was beginning to snow. Friends had come from Romania, the Director was present, although bristling a little, and we were joined by neighbours, relatives and friends, including many of our Gideon friends and many of the church members. One had the sense of diabolic opposition in the background, and yet an overwhelming certainty that the Lord is victor.

In the middle of the service the electricity failed, but this had little effect on the proceedings. Pastor Hughes preached on "Joy in heaven over one sinner who repents" (Luke 15:7). Many spoke, including the mayor, who incurred the wrath of the Director for referring to the six women as "poor things"!

There were a number of mothers of children with disabilities present, one of whom spoke, warmly commending the work. The six women sang and received many small gifts and cards. Tanea was present and some of Liliana's relatives. It was the most wonderful opportunity to praise the God of heaven for His wonderful works to the children of men. We counted ourselves blessed indeed to see such things and to be part of such a day. It became our Hallelujah day.

The next day we accompanied the women from Casa Bucuriei to church for the first time. The church in Truşeni is but a short walk, down a muddy trackway, from the house. In those days there was an old wood stove to heat the church. The building is old and that morning it was full, with brothers and sisters from Moldova, Romania and Wales. It is a most warm fellowship of saints. There are many older women who have lived through times of great hardship and suffering. Some lost their husbands in times of bitter persecution. But there are many who know what it is to prevail with the Lord in prayer. Outwardly, they look insignificant and poor—layers of garments to cope with the cold, a large patterned scarf covering their heads and weather-beaten, wrinkled faces. But the Lord is everything to them and they live with their eyes on the glory to be revealed. The young people in the church had prepared songs in Romanian, Russian and English for us. The women from Casa Bucuriei were asked to participate and did so with the most enormous pleasure. They sang their hearts out and we praised God from the depths of our souls. Many preached or spoke with power. We had not words to express our thankfulness to God. After we had enjoyed a splendid lunch at Casa Bucuriei the day ended with some of us attending the service at one of the large churches in Chișinău. Next morning our visitors returned to their own countries and we were left to ponder on all that we had witnessed.

Later that week we returned to the institution to see the women we had left behind. We spoke to many of them, including blind Lilia who quoted the verses from Matthew 25:37 onwards to me: "Lord, when did we see You hungry and feed You, or thirsty and give You drink? When did we see You a stranger and take You in ...?"

We were summoned to see the Director and the meeting began ominously. She was in a thunderous mood again but thankfully our discussion ended well. She said that she trusted us and that she thought we were "good people" because we believed in God. Once again she sought assurances that the women would be well provided for. Many times, we have talked to her about our Saviour and the fact that the Lord is the One to whom we look for all our needs. Many times we have prayed for her. When later she became furiously opposed to our work, I talked to Liliana about praying that the Lord would remove her from her post and give us someone more sympathetically disposed to the Gospel. Liliana very gently rebuked me, saying that we should pray instead for God's abundant blessing on her life and for him to draw her to himself in great love and mercy. She was right.

12

A Spiritual Work

... this is the gate of heaven!
(Genesis 28:17)

April 2007: we were speeding from Casa Bucuriei to
Anea's small flat, taking two of the women from Casa
Bucuriei to stay with us in the city for the week-end.
The stars were shining brilliantly in the indigo sky above us
and, suddenly, I was aware that we had the most precious
cargo with us and that we were surrounded by a heavenly
host.

That morning I had been reading again the story of Jacob's
dream at Bethel and how he had awoken and said, "This
is none other than the house of God, and this the gate of
heaven!" (Genesis 28:17) I had been sleeping at Casa Bucuriei
that night and had been unable to get to sleep because of

the cold. The night was lit by a brilliant moon and clear stars which flooded my room with light. It was always very quiet in the village at night. The only sound was the faint chiming of the bells from the Orthodox church opposite our house when they moved in the wind. I meditated on the words I had read that day. As I contemplated everything I could see in Casa Bucuriei, I had no difficulty at all in understanding that this was the "house of God". Every single thing in this house, from each brick to each piece of furniture, had been provided by the abundant goodness and provision of our God—of that there was no question. But what did "the gate of heaven" mean? Of course, we wanted the women all to be saved and, as far as we could see, three of them were evidently the Lord's. They had been converted whilst still living in the institution. The other three had an interest in spiritual things but there was no clear evidence that they were the Lord's. We longed that all of them should truly know Him.

There was another hurdle in our Moldovan context. It was the expectation that those who sincerely wanted to repent of their sins and follow Christ should make a public profession of faith before the church. How often I had seen this happen in the large church we normally attended in the city. It seemed at the end of most morning services a crowd of people of all ages would come to the front of the church before the service ended. They would kneel and pray, publicly confessing their sins and asking the Lord to rescue them and to have mercy on them. In those days, especially in the 1990s, many people were turning to the Lord and it was thrilling to see the Lord's hand at work, mighty to save. When we listened to the preached Word it so often came with great power and created an earnest desire in all of us to repent and put right the things that were wrong in our lives, so that we could live more holy lives. Time and again the Word has come with such convicting authority to my heart and soul, showing me my sin so clearly and causing me to rush to the Saviour for forgiveness and cleansing.

The preachers were not always great theologians of the kind I was so accustomed to at home, and they were not always particularly well instructed in prestigious schools of theology. Some of the older pastors had had little opportunity to go to Bible colleges. Their messages did not usually follow an expositional theme, which continued for a period of time, but tended to be "one off" messages on a certain text of Scripture. But they preached their hearts out and everybody knew that the Lord was with us of a certainty. We did not want them to stop preaching; we could have listened all day and all night. It was sometimes as if the Lord had touched their tongues with a coal of fire from off the altar. They preached with "all boldness" and with a directness that was most evident. The realities of heaven and hell were presented to congregations in a way that compelled us to think on things unseen and caused us to see the most awful plight of a soul without God.

When I had worked in Romania, the Lord had brought me into contact with many people who had lived through a time of recent revival. Many of them had also known great persecution under Ceausescu and communism. I called these people whose lives had been touched by "celestial fire", from Charles Wesley's great hymn:

O Thou who camest from above
The pure celestial fire to impart

I saw this same celestial fire amongst many of the saints in Moldova—lives on fire for God, with His Word burning in their hearts. In Moldova, in the years following the fall of the Soviet Union, it was not uncommon to attend a baptismal service where over a hundred people were being baptised, and these services would be held several times a year. Many churches were crammed full of people at services and a number would stand throughout the lengthy services, in order to hear the Word preached. There was a generation famished for God's Word and so hungry in their pursuit of God. I have often heard from friends in Moldova that immediately following the revolution there were a multitude of young men and women on fire to bring the Gospel to their country.

In Casa Bucuriei there was an expectation of a similar public confession of faith and we could not imagine how these women that we knew and loved could ever find it within themselves to profess their love for the Saviour in such a way. It seemed to us to be an unnecessary ordeal for them and something that would never be within their capacity to countenance.

The day after my reflections on Jacob's dream was a Sunday. It happened that, unknown to us, an evangelistic meeting had been arranged in the church in Truşeni. In the afternoon we all went to the meeting which was to take place in the courtyard outside the small church. Although it was April the weather was still cold and we tried to sit in the sunshine to thaw our frozen bodies a little. There were

microphones fixed up outside and I wondered whatever the
neighbours must have thought to hear such loud volume
singing and preaching echoing forth all over the village. It
was not long before nearly all the seats in the courtyard were
full. The preacher was a pastor from one of the big churches
in the city. It transpired that he had been a theological
student in Oradea when I had been there in the 1990s. He
started to preach on John 3:16 ("For God so loved the world
that He gave His only begotten Son, that whoever believes
in Him should not perish but have everlasting life"). He
preached simply but very powerfully.

At the end of the service the pastor said that anyone to
whom God had spoken, and who wanted to talk over things
further with him, should come to the vestry inside the
church afterwards. Then he prayed. As I opened my eyes,
I could hardly understand what was happening. Anişoara
and Aliona were dashing across the courtyard in front of
me, making for the vestry with Vera, Nastea and Serafima
following. Diana was left shouting in her wheelchair, "Don't
forget me! I want to speak to him too!" Aliona and Anişoara
rapidly came to her rescue and wheeled her into the vestry.
We found ourselves all sitting in the low-ceilinged small
room which served as the vestry. There was an old wooden
table in the centre behind which was sitting the pastor who
had just preached, whilst we perched on wooden benches
round the wall of the room. In the gentle discussion which
followed it became clear that the Lord had spoken clearly to
each of our friends from Casa Bucuriei. The three women
who were already converted—Diana, Aliona and Anişoara—
wanted to make a public declaration of their existing
faith, whilst Vera, Nastea and Serafima had clearly found

newly-given faith in the Saviour. We did not have words to adequately express our joy. As we returned to Casa Bucuriei and celebrated with a special tea together, the words "and this is the gate of heaven!" (Genesis 28:17) came back to me with a fresh clarity.

It was inconceivable that the Lord would have left a work half-finished. He, who had prepared a way out of the institution for these women and had given them a home and a church that received them with much love, showed His determination to save each one and prepare them for glory. It was a day of great rejoicing for all of us. As the months went by and we observed the lives of the women, we knew that the work was a real one.

Living and working in Moldova, and previously in Romania, has had a profound effect on me spiritually. When I first went to live in Romania I was very back-slidden as a Christian. Outwardly, I kept up with the formalities of church attendance and reading my Bible and praying, but there was a deep rebellion in my heart and a meddling with this world which did my soul no good. What took me by great surprise was that, instead of giving me my just deserts in terms of chastisement, the Lord took me into a context of great spiritual blessing. Such is His great grace that He so rewards sinners! He weaned me back with blessing.

Although there is a day-to-day drudgery about living in some Eastern European countries, and a harshness to everyday life, where I was living spiritual realities were very much clearer than at home. That was true both in Oradea, in Romania, and now in Moldova. I have compared it to putting on a pair of spectacles. As someone who is short-sighted, if I have a speaking engagement I will usually remove my glasses so that I cannot see my listeners. Without my glasses the faces of everyone who is in the congregation will be blurred and indistinct, thus relieving my nerves. That is sometimes how I feel about spiritual life in our country at the moment. For example, those glorious realities of "every spiritual blessing in the heavenly places in Christ" (Ephesians 1:3) or "the exceeding greatness of His power toward us who believe" (Ephesians 1:19) are blurred by our unbelief and the allurement of this world. We can spend a long time talking with fellow believers, but never talk about Him. Our conversation is too often full of the trifling little pleasures of this world, or complaints about trivial things. It is as if we are living in a spiritual fog.

When I am living with friends in Moldova, it is as if I have put on a new pair of spiritual spectacles. Of course, we will never have 20/20 spiritual vision as long as we are on this earth, but there are situations in which we can see spiritual things more acutely and with greater precision. So there, heaven and hell come into sharper relief, and the most transient nature of everything we see here is more apparent. Many of my Christian friends in Moldova long for heaven and for the Lord's second coming and eagerly wait for these things. I can remember, some years ago, that a good friend there linked my arm as we walked along a very dark street at night. Times were very difficult economically then for many people, and there were real hardships. But she said to me, "But He is coming soon—and what joy there will be then!" Their preoccupation is with things unseen, not with the idols of this world which can so devour our energies in the West.

There was an almost imperceptible effect on my soul of things that I had witnessed in Moldova and Romania.

1 A lake in Sofia in summer

2 Anea (1980)

3 Anea's parents (1963)

4 Left to right: Anea, Valea, Tanea and Dora
(1980)

Photos

6 A Park in Chişinău

5 Tanea (1980)

7 A well in Truşeni

8 A well in Sofia

9 A sleigh ride with Petru, Slava and
Gheorghe

10 Giving out food in an institution (1)

11 Giving out food in an institution (2)

12 Giving out food in an institution (3)

Photos

13 An open-air meeting at summer camp in an institution

14 Two friends at an institution

15 Sasha

16 A Gospel meeting in an institution (1)

17 A Gospel meeting in an institution (2)

18 Casa Alex and Casa Matei—a birthday gathering

19 Casa Alex

20 Casa Matei

Photos

21 Foundations and well for the fourth house
at Căpriana

22 Gheorghe (Casa Matei) and Pete Nye

23 Left to right: Gheorghe, Petru and Slava at
Casa Matei

24 Casa Bucuriei: Left to right (top): Vera,
Aliona, Anişoara Left to right (front row):
Diana, Nastea and Serafima

25 Opening of Casa Alex, August 27th 2011

26 Monastery at Căpriana

27 Moldovan village house

28 Reads 'I love Moldova'

Photos

29 Sora Lena and Liliana

30 Tanea (2014)

31 Maureen, Liliana and Anea

32 Marinela, Maureen and Liliana in Oradea (2014)

33 A church in Chişinău

I noticed it only over a long period of time. My appetite for this world had dulled. Although I still rejoiced in the indescribable beauty of God's creation and knew that I was most blessed by so many good things He had given me, precious friends included, the pull that this world used to have on my life diminished a little. I began to feel that I had spent so much of my Christian life chasing trivia, not necessarily obviously sinful things but things that took up too much of my time and attention, but were of no real profit. I remembered Amy Carmichael's description of Christians being busy making daisy chains as they sat near the edge of a cliff, seeing people walking towards the cliff edge and doing nothing to warn them of their dreadful danger. And I recalled one of her poems that I had learnt long ago:

> *From prayer that asks that I may be*
> *Sheltered from winds that beat on Thee,*
> *From fearing when I should aspire,*
> *From faltering when I should climb higher,*
> *From silken self, O Captain, free*
> *Thy soldier who would follow Thee.*
>
> *From subtle love of softening things,*
> *From easy choices, weakenings,*
> *(Not thus are spirits fortified,*
> *Not this way went the Crucified)*
> *From all that dims Thy Calvary,*
> *O Lamb of God, deliver me.*

The phrase "Not this way went the Crucified" sounded in

my soul when I found myself in questionable territory. I began to find contentment in the Lord Himself. I regretted spending so much time chasing other things when I could have been pursuing God, but I resolved, by His grace, to follow him in the time that was left to me.

The love of the Moldovan Christians I knew was powerfully evident. Such love! It was a love that accepted people for who they were, without being critical of them; it saw the best in them. This love persevered in times of difficulty and did not give up on others. It put others first all the time. It was a love that took delight in serving. There was nothing artificial about it. I have lived with Moldovans for long enough to see its authenticity. This was a love that came from heaven and breathed the Saviour's love for us. I saw graciousness in their attitude to people who treated them badly or rudely. It was the fragrance of Christ in a culture that was frequently tough and hostile.

My friends were people of great faith, which was vigorously exercised on a daily basis. These were a people who knew their God and were strong and did exploits. They had an experiential knowledge of God's glorious sovereignty. Life was lived in the knowledge that He was on the throne and whatever happened was taken as from the hand of a loving Father in heaven. This was true of painful as well as joyful providences. They trusted the God who had saved them with whatever circumstances through which He took them. This has spoken to me very much over the years. I had been used in my own country to knowing and hearing much about God's sovereignty in all things, but here I came face to face with Christians who demonstrated these wonderful truths in their behaviour. There was a lack of murmuring or complaining against God or others. Great thankfulness, praise and joy also characterised their walk with the Lord. Prayers and conversations were the expression of very thankful hearts. Not a day passes without my being aware of this in Moldova. It causes the soul to delight in the Lord and to go after the One who is "fairer that the sons of men" (Psalm 45:2) and who is "altogether lovely" (Song of Solomon 5:16) in our sight. He becomes our "exceeding joy" (Psalm 43:4).

13

The Institution in the North

I will make mention of Your righteousness, of Yours only
(Psalm 71:16)

I needed some English New Testaments for a class of students I was teaching. A sister who was very involved in the Gideon work in Chișinău said that she would be able to provide them and I went to collect them one afternoon. An attractive woman in her forties, with long, thick, curly hair and a beautiful smile, opened the door to a small flat and warmly invited me in. This was my first meeting with Lena who was to become my very good friend and a great help to us in our work.

Lena told me how she had been converted just five years previously, at her husband's baptismal service. She explained that a number of the Gideons and their wives had been visiting a large institution for adults with disabilities in the north of Moldova. She and her husband, Slava, had a particular interest in this institution for, apart from their daughter, Nastea, who was in her twenties, they had a teenaged son, Vasile, who has autism. They tried to visit the institution about four times a year, depending on whether there was enough money for the trips. It was a long journey and they prepared food to take with them for everybody living there. Lena got out a small photo album and began to show me photos of people they had met on their visits there. She told me that there were no organised activities there and few carers. Those living there would wear all their clothes, for fear of them being stolen. The photos showed people suffering abject neglect and deprivation—it was like seeing a modern day picture of a concentration camp. As I looked through the photo album I cried.

A few weeks later, Lena phoned to ask if we would like to accompany the Gideons on their next visit to this institution. We said we would like to go and very early indeed one Saturday morning we arrived at the big Russian church from which the transport was to leave. We arrived to a scene of tremendous activity. A large group of Russian-speaking men was packing a minibus with food and clothing. It seemed that Lena and another sister had been at the church all night, cooking an enormous amount of food to take with us. When everything was ready we all stood outside the minibus to pray. It was still dark and icy cold as we left. Everybody was wearing big, fur hats and their warmest jackets.

We sped northwards, through ever increasing snow and ice and sometimes fog. On our way we passed endless villages, with brightly painted houses and elaborately decorated gateways. Some of the houses had painted murals on their walls. Occasionally, we would stumble upon a large Orthodox church with shining gold domes, or a flock of sheep accompanied by a shepherd clad in a huge sheepskin and hat. After some time we stopped for a picnic in a heavily snow-laden forest by the side of the road. It was amazingly well organised—there were mugs of steaming hot, sweet, black tea and food that was still warm, in giant containers. I noticed that this group took every opportunity to pray for the day ahead of us. There was much laughter and I saw a very close bond between all of them.

Eventually we arrived at the village nearest to the institution. Someone pointed out the Director's house to me—it was a very large, impressive edifice on the edge of the village. The road, poor as it was, ended at the village and the rest of our journey, another four kilometres, was along what could barely be described as a track. Lena laughed as she told me of one occasion when their minibus had got inextricably stuck in deep snow and had to be hauled out by a tractor. In the distance, I could make out a number of low buildings, clustered together in the middle of nowhere. This was where we were heading. Huge gates and walls greeted us as we approached. Slava had driven us the last few kilometres, through deep snow and mud. We could see a number of men clinging to the bars of the gates on the inside as we got nearer. They were peering intently at the visitors. They were very poorly clothed. Some had shaved heads and I wondered how very cold they must have been without hats. A crowd gathered round us as soon as we entered and for the first time I saw some women amongst them. Many were clamouring for human contact and conversation and there was very great excitement as they realised that we had brought food with us. Some rushed indoors to alert everybody, and the crowd increased, both in size and volume.

There were clothes draped around the grounds, over chairs and walls. They must have been washed, but they still looked very dirty. The ice had frozen them into statuesque forms. The concrete building we entered first was grey and drab and there was a foul smell as we went inside. It was dark in the corridors. My memories of that visit are dominated by a sense of visiting endless rooms and seeing row upon row of men and women, sitting waiting for food. Some of them were cowering and many had cuts and bruises on their faces. The staff we saw seemed to keep some sort of control with cruelty. We heard them using a form of speech which peasants use for horses when they are giving them commands, much as I suppose the Nazis used for prisoners. In every room we gave out food, which those living there ate from tin bowls, with or without dirty spoons. I noticed that many hid some of their food inside their jumpers or jackets. It was a strange kind of feast: there was kasha (a kind of porridge), a sausage, a beetroot and an onion. Everybody had a small loaf and a banana and a chocolate wafer biscuit. Many voraciously wolfed the food down and some ate the banana skin. It was busy, going from room to room, trying to ensure that everybody was fed, but the suffering with which I was confronted there on that first visit almost overwhelmed me. I can remember silently praying for people as I gave them food.

I saw a number of people who clearly had Down's syndrome and some others with terrible physical disabilities.

There was one woman whose legs were somehow locked in a foetal position, but whose head was permanently hanging down from the bed; it seemed that she would even eat in this position. Beds were crowded together in every huge room, most with very little bedding. My Gideon friends were later to tell me that the beds were a relatively recent acquisition, and that previously, people had been sleeping on thin mattresses on the floor or on the concrete itself. There were people who were clearly too ill to do other than spend all their time in bed. Some of those living there had no obvious disability at all. They were brought there simply because they had no family, or had been rejected by relatives. I talked to one man, probably in his fifties, who told me that his family had abandoned him there. He said he had brothers in Chișinău and he asked me if I would contact them on his behalf. I said that I would. When people died there, he told me, as frequently they did, the other inmates had to carry the bodies and bury them themselves in a communal grave. In every room we entered hands reached out to us to attract our attention, or to say, "Buna ziua"—"Good day." We were introduced to a handful of doctors, themselves shabbily dressed. Most of them looked indifferent and hard. It could hardly have been a desirable occupation to be working in such an isolated location, with so few resources.

All of us were deeply affected by the visit. On the way home, we stopped again in a white forest for a hot meal, which appeared amazingly from some big containers we had in the van. We prayed at some length before eating. Most of the Gideon brothers were strong, hefty men with hearty appetites and the food disappeared quickly. As time went on I was to learn more of their individual histories and the Lord's dealings with them, but then I realised only that I had come into contact with a group of men and women who were very strong in the Lord Jesus and who were being spent out for him. They talked about their first visits to the institution in the North. On their very first visit they had seen people out in the snow with no shoes on and very little in the way of clothing. They were eating slops and fish entrails and drinking only water. There had only been one bowl of cold water to wash about thirty people. Some were sleeping on bare cement floors.

I can remember sitting in Anea's car as we arrived back at our apartment block late in the evening. We spoke of all that the Lord had given us in terms of warmth and food and clothing and people who cared about us and how very thankful we were. We talked about the situation of those we had met in the institution that day with such heavy hearts. But again, we could not forget them and the memory of what we had seen would not erase itself from our minds. We began to pray for them.

The following months and years provided very precious times of fellowship and work with our Gideon friends. One evening there was quite a crowd of us gathered round Anea's table and people began to talk about their experiences under communism. Volodya, one of the Gideon leaders, recounted how his father had been one of the Baptist bishops in Moldova. He had been killed by the KGB, who had given him injections over a long period of time that progressively and irreparably damaged his body. Volodya and his wife lived in a rough area of the city, but had had great opportunities to witness to neighbours. One of their neighbours had been Slava's mother, who was one of the first to be converted.

After that Slava had become a Christian, and then Lena, although she had been very opposed for a while to the Gospel and her husband's conversion.

Sister Raisa, an older Christian, spoke of many she knew who had been sent to labour camps in Siberia or to prison. She was a godly woman of very great faith. Once I heard her praying in the big Russian church with all the fervency of a soul on fire for God. She and the others all said that under communism their faith had been "fierbinte"'—"boiling hot" and they had been much in prayer for each other. They said that was not true of them now in the same way. For me, it was as if I had been brought into contact with Christians who *were* "boiling hot" in comparison to how I knew ourselves to be in the UK, and I reflected on the quality of their Christian lives as they must have been when facing persecution. It was such a benediction to spend time with them, speaking about the Lord and praying together.

Most of them belonged to one of the big Russian churches in the city at the time. One of the brothers showed me the inside of their church early one morning before we left for the institution in the north of Moldova. He wept as he recounted how they had built the church during some of the worst days of communism. It was a very large, most beautiful building with a huge balcony upstairs and seating for about two thousand people. I later learnt the history of the construction of this remarkable edifice and saw many fascinating photos of those who had been involved in the building work. For many years the congregation of Russian-speaking Moldovans had been trying to obtain permission from the Communist authorities to build a "prayer house." Their former meeting place was in a deplorable state as the result of an earthquake which had rendered it unsafe. Eventually, and after much prayer, they were given authorisation to build. The choice of an actual construction site caused many difficulties. The church members proposed a number of potential sites, but each was rejected by the authorities. The objection was that they were too near other buildings, such as a school, or buildings with cultural purposes, and the presence of a church might "contaminate" its environs. Finally, a piece of land on the outskirts of the town, which was inhabited only by goats and geese, was accepted by the Communists as suitable.

Having agreed the location, the Communist officials then proceeded to communicate detailed instructions about the law as it related to the construction of "cult" places of worship. Amongst these instructions were rulings that the members had to construct the church with their own hands and with their own finances. They were forbidden to receive any assistance from other churches and if it was discovered that they had received any assistance from abroad, those responsible would be punished under the penal code. They were not allowed to use any technical equipment in the construction—this meant that it had literally to be built by hand. If there was any breach at all in the conditions laid down, the right to build a church would be removed permanently. Every attempt was being made to tie their hands and make the project impossible to realise. Although ostensibly permission had been given to go ahead, so many impediments were put in the way that the officials planned that the project would fall at the first hurdle. The church leaders listened to the conditions which had been laid down, but told the authorities that they would continue to build, because their hope and their faith was in God. They were sure that He would help them.

The work began. On 28th February 1983, at 9am, there was a reading from the Scriptures, and prayer, and the labourers began their task. The members began to look for construction materials they needed in shops that sold such materials in Chișinău and throughout Moldova. But the shop-holders had already received instructions from the Communist Party that they were not to sell any such materials to the Baptists. After much prayer, the church leaders began to look for construction materials in neighbouring republics and they began to see a miracle unfold. The brothers spoke to the director of a shop in a republic bordering Moldova and showed him the Government papers authorising the construction. The director ordered his workers to provide the very best materials for the Christians, as they were preparing to build the house of God. There was a service of thanksgiving when the first brick was laid and there was a message from a text of Scripture in Zechariah: "The hands of Zerubbabel have laid the foundation of this temple; his hands shall also finish it. Then you will know that the Lord of Hosts has sent Me to you" (Zechariah 4:9–10).

To the undisguised amazement of the authorities and the citizens of Chișinău, the building began to take shape, albeit with the most primitive methods of construction. Young and old church members, men and women, all took their places in labouring, day and night, on the new building. It was a most formidable task, in the absence of the most basic equipment needed to build. Many of the bricks had to be hand-made. The state authorities continually tried to find occasions for proving that the church members had broken the legislation, but they were unable to find the grounds necessary. Spies repeatedly attempted to denounce them for supposed infractions. People offered them building materials in order to trap them, but God always gave them wisdom to discern those whose intention was to harm them. There were false accusations in the newspapers that "the Baptists have abandoned their jobs to build a prayer house." The reality was that they were completing this work in addition to their ordinary jobs. The electricity was regularly disconnected deliberately. On one very difficult occasion, a petition to stop the construction work was presented to the judiciary. The members were confronted by opposition from the locality, the town officials and the Government. The case was discussed even in Moscow, where anti-religious propaganda had drawn unwanted attention. The Moldovan authorities realised that they had made a big mistake granting building permission in the first place. But, quite miraculously, the work went on.

Moscow sent an official to ascertain what more devious, outwardly legitimate, means might be found to prevent the construction work continuing. He held a secret meeting with local Communist officials to discuss this. A loophole was identified. There were two Baptist prayer houses in Chișinău and, according to the legislation, a religious community could not have two prayer houses. The new school year was fast approaching. It was proposed that it would be good for the town authorities to make a present of the growing church building to the children of the city and for it to become a Pioneer House (the Pioneers were the young people's branch of the Communist Party). The church leaders hurriedly prepared the papers finalising the use of the building—it was the middle of August and the school year was due to begin on 1st September. One of the minor Party officials, much like Nicodemus, met one of the church leaders in secret, as he was so indignant at some of the injustices which were occurring and so impressed by the work of the church members. He advised them to occupy the new premises as their official prayer house without delay, even though the building was not complete. Thus, the final service took place in the old building, and a members' meeting decided that they should move into the new church the next day. The members fasted and prayed; they felt the Lord so very close to them and were greatly encouraged in Him. God did not allow their enemies to triumph.

The building work was characterised by fervent, daily prayer on behalf of the members and their Christian brothers and sisters throughout Moldova, by extremely hard physical labour, to which the whole church was committed, and most of all by the ongoing miracles of God. In 1986 the work was completed and there was a service of dedication. The first service of baptism took place on 7th October. It was thrilling to realise that some of my new Russian-speaking friends had been eyewitnesses of this most incredible work of God.

Outreach to People with Disabilities

... as having nothing, and yet possessing all things
(2 Corinthians 6:10)

Lena and Slava became particularly dear to me. Like so many I met they had been converted relatively recently, but already they were fully committed to the Lord's service and full of a zeal given by the Holy Spirit. They counted no sacrifice too great for Him and were earnest in their efforts to win others to their new-found Saviour. I can clearly remember a party at their small flat, to celebrate Lena's fortieth birthday. My birthday greetings in Russian had been well practised. The flat was already full when we arrived and a tremendous display of food covered the table. Most of those present were involved in the work of the Gideons. When Lena rose to give thanks for the food we all rose with her to pray. Grace is no cursory prayer in Moldova and Lena prayed and praised God at length, but as she did so it was another occasion when heaven drew near again and we were taken into the presence of the Lord. After eating and talking a great deal we began to sing Russian hymns—wonderful old hymns, all in the minor key and with four-part accompaniment. We reluctantly left, late that night, and were enveloped in the dark snowy conditions outside.

Our visits to the large institution in the north continued, sometimes with the Gideons, but sometimes just Anea, Liliana and I would go, when we had time. Lena would try to come with us as often as she could. Her heart was in the work and she longed for a better future for her friends there. Sometimes, she told me, she was so upset by what she saw there that she was unable to eat for some time after visiting. She would think about her own son and could not help imagining what his life would have been like if he had ever gone to such a place to live. The need to open a house for some of the men she had got to know there was continually on her heart.

Soon after our first visit we accompanied the Gideons again, with Lena and Slava among them, on their next visit. It was like arriving at a modern day Bedlam. The noise level was at mega decibels; many of the inmates had cuts and bruises on their faces and many were very sick. A large number had shaven heads. All were wearing their outdoor clothing, including scarves and hats, for fear that these might be stolen and because they had nowhere else to put their things. As we went through the institution giving out food we were accompanied by a young woman inmate who was wielding a knife and who was screaming orders at everyone. It made for a scene of utter chaos. Lena introduced me to two young men with Down's syndrome— Petru and Slava. Petru was probably in his twenties and was thin and unkempt, with a glazed, depressed look. He seemed not to be able to speak, but pointed at our warm clothing and then at his very inadequate clothing. We gave him some warmer clothes but I cried as I considered his situation.

We were introduced to Zina. She looked about fifty years old and was unable to walk. She was sitting in what appeared to be a cupboard, or a very tiny room, where it seemed she spent nearly all her time. Her very warm greetings to us were hard to comprehend when one thought about the desperateness of her circumstances. On this occasion we also met one of the women whom we had known well from the other institution we had visited, from which the women in Casa Bucuriei had come. Her name was Olga and she had been sent here, so it was said, because of her aggressive behaviour and bad language. We were shocked by the change in her appearance. Her face was bloated with crying and her eyes were very red. She had marks on her body which, she said, had been inflicted by beatings from others living there. Olga pleaded with us to take her back to her former home; she said that she would beg forgiveness of the Director on her knees and would never cause her any problems again. She clung to us with a truly piteous grief and pleaded with us to intercede on her behalf. We later did so, but to no effect. With time, as we visited on future occasions, Olga's reaction to us became slightly muted—we thought as the result of sedative medication. Her situation had a deep effect on all of us and was one of the reasons why we determined to visit this place regularly.

As my friendship with Lena and Slava grew I heard more about the work of the Gideons in Moldova. Here were a group of men and women who sometimes distributed a thousand New Testaments in a day and who were thoroughly committed to regular visiting of hospitals, prisons, and numerous other places with words of love and bold testimony. Lena told me of a recent situation where the doctor on a local hospital ward had asked to see one of the lady Gideons. He told Lena of a patient in agony who was not being helped either by medication or by injections. Lena gave the patient a New Testament and spoke to him of the Lord. Patients on his ward took it in turns, at his request, to read the New Testament right through to him. He said that his pain had eased. By the morning he had died, but he was found with the New Testament clasped to his chest and he was smiling.

From a little further afield, Slava told me of a Russian officer who had been captured by Chechen rebels. He had been taken out several times to be shot, but the actual execution had never happened—it was a form of psychological torture. He was beaten very badly and his feet were broken and he was left for dead. He was left lying next to a heap of rubbish. On top of the rubbish were some pages from the New Testament, which he managed to grasp. There was another soldier lying near to him who was also badly injured. The officer asked him if he knew the Lord's Prayer. He said that he did and they repeated it over and over again.

Some Russian soldiers eventually rescued them. The Russian officer was converted a little later. He left the army and is now an active Gideon.

From the beginning of the work at Casa Bucuriei Lena and Slava had been a great support and encouragement to us. They were present at the opening service and visited the house regularly, subsequently becoming very good friends of the women who live there. Vasile always accompanied them and, despite his fears about meeting strangers and being in new situations, he soon became very used to being with us and was clearly happy in our company. One day Lena invited me, with a friend, to attend a meeting of mothers of children with disabilities which was being held in Chișinău. My friend had herself adopted two children with disabilities and was asked to share a little of her experience. There was a surprisingly large number of mothers present and there was a lot of lively participation. Some spoke of the Lord's help in their situation, but not all professed a personal faith. It was obvious that they were all struggling with a dreadful lack of support of any kind from society, but were determined to provide the very best quality of care for their offspring against all the odds. I was very impressed by both their courage and tenacity. Here was a group of women who found themselves in a society that had little to offer anybody with a disability, who wanted to change things not only for themselves but for others.

As a mother of a child with a disability herself, Lena was readily accepted by the group and she took a leading part in its activities. But Lena wanted more, and Slava supported her in this. Their profound desire was that these families would come to know the Saviour. Ever a dynamic activist,

Lena was involved in helping with a summer evangelistic camp for these mothers and their children of whatever age. Individuals with disabilities, who did not necessarily have family support, would also be welcome. Lena and Slava realised very clearly that these mothers very frequently had little, if any, respite from their caring roles. They were often worn down with sleepless nights and continual labours and would benefit both from being with other mothers who understood the pressures, and by a change of environment.

Lena and Slava began to pray and asked others to join them in this. Having no material means at their disposal to embark on such a venture made little difference to them. And the first camp took place early one autumn. An evangelist, Brother Dima, who is himself disabled, preached during the week. Very many mothers and some fathers and their children of all ages attended, delighted to have the opportunity for a break from the day-to-day drudgery of their existence. Some were believers, but many were not. All knew that this was to be a Christian camp. It turned out to be a time of tremendous blessing for those who attended. Christians were greatly encouraged and some mothers and children were converted. It was a time of very great happiness and rejoicing. The Lord had honoured the desire of Lena and Slava to encourage these families and to bring them into the presence of the Saviour. It was to be the first of many such camps.

Brother Dima has a remarkable ministry. In 1978 he fell out of a tree and sustained a spinal injury. Shortly after this, he came to know the Lord and was given a burning desire to share his faith with others. He uses a wheelchair and for the last few years he has been given an adapted car which he uses in his ministry to other people with disabilities. Once I had the opportunity to spend a day with him. Despite his disability he is the kind of person who seems to know absolutely everybody. In the market-place crowds of people came up to the car to greet him warmly. He spoke to so many about the Lord and distributed Christian literature to each one. He took us to meet a number of disabled Christians, all living in most difficult circumstances. One such was a young man, Vitali, then aged twenty-eight, who has cerebral palsy and was also a wheelchair user. We travelled a long way on treacherous roads to see him and joked about having arrived at what felt like "caputul lumei"—"the end of the earth."

Vitali's house was a miserable hovel, with a roof that was collapsing and huge steps to the front door, which seemed impossible for him to access. The house was surrounded by a small, neglected garden. We could not get an answer at Vitali's home and the front door was padlocked. Some neighbours told us that he was staying with his sister in Ghurguleşti. Brother Dima knew that Vitali's sister, who was not a Christian, often took his very small income for herself and that he was not really wanted in her home. We travelled on to Ghurguleşti. Vitali came out of his sister's house to greet us and his sister quickly followed, trying to see if we had brought anything of value for Vitali. She and her husband left after a time as they were attending a wedding, and we had the opportunity to spend precious time with Vitali on his own. The Lord had done a remarkable work in his life. When one considered the poverty of his circumstances, in every sense, and his dependence on others to a large extent, it was a depressing picture. Vitali had a hacking cough which made me wonder if he, like so many others in Moldova, had tuberculosis. However, the young man who met us was full of joy. It seemed almost incomprehensible, until we remembered the Saviour from whom Vitali derived that joy. Vitali explained that he had been praying for provisions that very morning. He said he had been reading those verses in Luke: "Consider the lilies, how they grow: they neither toil nor spin; and yet I say to you, even Solomon in all his glory was not arrayed like one of these ... And do not seek what you should eat or what you should drink, nor have an anxious mind ... your Father knows that you need these things" (Luke 12:27, 29–30). We were standing in the road outside his sister's house. Brother Dima was in the car in the driver's seat and reached to hold Vitali's hand as he sat in a wheelchair alongside the car. Vitali began to pray and as he praised God our hearts were filled with the presence and the joy of the Lord. It was an unforgettable encounter. Brother Dima spoke to Vitali at length, encouraging him from the Word and we were able to leave some food and clothing supplies with him.

We spent the day visiting disabled Christians in a number of isolated villages. Some had been converted at the camp and it was wonderful to hear their testimonies. All were struggling with huge difficulties in day-to-day living. But it was not these things that preoccupied their conversation; they wanted fellowship and they wanted to talk about the Lord who had given them peace with God. Dima's ministry was a benediction to them.

Another of the Christians who had been much helped by the camp was Victor. He lived with his eighty-one year-old father, and his sister and her three young children. None of his relatives were Christians. He also had cerebral palsy and his "home" was an alcove near the window of their little cottage, where he spent most of his time. Victor rarely got out as he needed a lot of help to get into his wheelchair, and that help was not often available. He shared how he had been converted eleven years previously at a tent mission in his village. The Orthodox Church opposed the mission fiercely and one day the priest and some other men set fire to the tent to prevent the work continuing. They came to Victor's house to sprinkle holy water everywhere to rid Victor of the "demonic influences". But the Lord had saved him powerfully and no opposition would move him from his new-found Saviour. Victor had attended the first camp and was immeasurably blessed by the fellowship and the spiritual encouragement he found there.

At the end of a long, tiring day Brother Dima invited us back to his home in Cahul. The house was in darkness as we arrived, but his wife came out to meet us. We watched as she expertly lifted her husband out of the car into the wheelchair, taking his full body weight. She explained that she had done this for many years and was very used to carrying him, but we and she realised that there would be a time when she would no longer be able to do this—the couple were in their forties. The courtyard was crammed with wheelchairs and other equipment that Brother Dima distributed to those in need; he had acquired these from a German mission. Later, as we left, we prayed together in the dark street outside their house and felt that we had met with some of God's choice servants that day.

First Camp and
the Second House

He made the stars also
(Genesis 1:16)

It was August 2008 and our first summer camp at the large institution in the north of the country. We were a multi-national team of about twenty, speaking three languages between us. The camp site was an unusual one in that we had pitched on a narrow strip of rough ground by the side of a track leading down to the institution. We had had to hack down a huge array of weeds to make room for the tents and uncovered a large ant mound (which we avoided) and a veritable maze of mole hills (over which we camped). The mole hills proved to be a source of constant amusement to us as new mounds were thrown up, both within and outside our tents, at all times of day and night. There was a rubbish dump in close proximity. Very occasionally vehicles would pass, throwing up dust clouds in their wake, but more often a cart and horse would meander past our improvised site, with the driver agog to discover the inhabitants of this strange tented dwelling place. Further up the track from where we had camped a most beautiful view opened up above a nearby lake, with gentle hills rolling away on every side and wild flowers carpeting the ground. A heat haze gathered over the landscape as the day unravelled, merging everything into a dreamy mistiness.

The days were hot and filled with activity of all kinds. We were wakened early each morning to the sound of shouting and screaming in the distance from the institution. These same sounds echoed far into the nights also, often accompanied by the beat of very loud music. We realised that there could be no escape for those living there from the constant intrusion of such disturbances.

That first week was most blessed. We knew the presence of Emmanuel, "God with us," as we went into the institution each morning to befriend those who lived there and to share the Gospel. But one of the over-riding memories that remains with me is of the night sky that displayed its glory above us at the end of each day. There was no danger of light pollution, rough camping in the middle of nowhere as we were, and the dark dome above us revealed a multitude of stars and nocturnal activity such as I had never seen before. We would gaze at it in wonder before retiring. From the circle of the horizon all around us, up to the very heights of the dome above us, was an indescribable treasure trove of celestial beauty. In a small patch of that sky, wherever we looked, was an innumerable mass of stars. The Milky Way soared overhead in a huge streak of white dazzle. Shooting stars appeared and trail blazed their way across a path of darkness. Constellations showed themselves in all their glory, unmistakeable in their splendour. The sight, for all of us who saw it at that camp, was awesome. And I meditated on the One who had created this most compelling display of wonders. I remembered that sublime understatement in Genesis "He made the stars also" (Genesis 1:16). Psalm 147 reminds us that "He counts the number of the stars; He calls them all by name" (Psalm 147:4). Psalm 33 shows us that "By the word of the Lord the heavens were made, and all the host of them by the breath of His mouth" (Psalm 33:6). As I reflected on these things I began to see again that it was foolishness itself not to believe that with God all things are possible. We could trust him with very much greater things than we had already seen.

Despite a fair amount of initial chaos, the camp quickly took shape. There is a motley collection of memories: silence descending on the crowd when Andrei, a friend from Romania, spoke on the verse, "Silver and gold I do not have, but what I do have I give you" (Acts 3:6); the genuine enjoyment of many at the craft and sports activities; Nadia, always longing to snatch the microphone to sing one of the Christian songs she knew at the very top of her voice (and sometimes quickly afterwards hitting somebody fiercely!)

Vanya and Vitali and Gheorghe sheltered under the shade of the trees during the meetings, quietly listening with pleasure. Vanya and Vitali would persuade friends to wheel them up to our camp site in the evenings, where we gave them food and spoke to them of the Lord. Vanya is in his forties, has no legs, and has cerebral palsy. He is the Lord's and we knew that he had been baptised in the church in Sofia. Vanya has bright blue eyes and a huge smile, despite the pain he often has to endure. He needs assistance with many tasks but had a very good friend in Gheorghe, who fed him and wheeled him wherever he wanted to go. Vitali was twenty-two and has an undiagnosed degenerative condition which has led to the rapid loss of use of his legs, followed by an increasing lack of strength in his arms. He was abandoned by his family because of his condition when he was eighteen, and arrived at this institution. Vitali's face is often sad and pensive. He is intellectually able and gifted in drawing and painting, but has had to cope with rejection, cruelty, neglect and the deterioration of his physical abilities. These had brought him to the point where one felt that he had lost all hope. The Lord spoke to him during that summer camp and we witnessed his repentance and faith in the Lord Jesus.

Often another member of the team and I would visit those inside the institution who were unable to get to our meetings outside. There were some distressing scenes, We spoke to a man who had lost his legs in a very cold winter two years previously, and there was Fedya, whose body was hunched up in dirty bedclothes and who never left that bed. We saw neglect of pain, and untreated sores and sickness. It was sometimes difficult to distinguish the staff from those who lived there. Abuse and cruelty abounded. And yet into such a place the Lord had brought the Gospel and the presence of the Saviour of the world.

During one of the evenings we were invited to a church

in nearby Soroca. The congregation was mixed Moldovan and Roma and there was an elderly pastor who cried when he spoke of brothers who had gone through great suffering in the past. I discovered later that he had passed through such experiences also. He was full of praise to God for the freedom they had now been given. We knew great joy in that service and afterwards the congregation invited us to a simple meal with them. The room filled with the beautiful sound of their Russian songs of thanksgiving. We were so very glad to be there.

The week of the camp came to an end and we were travelling home to Chișinău, exhausted, but full of thanksgiving to God. En route, we had decided to stop at Sofia, a village about forty kilometres away from our camp, to view a house we had seen previously. We had been thinking and praying for some time about the possibility of buying a second house, particularly for some of the men from the institution where we had just been. The first time I had earlier seen what was to become Casa Matei, I had loved this house. In my mind there was something Tolstoyan about the place. It was a single-storey dwelling, with brightly coloured blue and amber external walls, light, high ceilinged rooms with the usual "soba" or wood burning stove, a vine outside which provided welcome shelter from the sun and the most beautiful lake a few steps from the bottom of the most enormous garden.

There were some links already formed between the village of Sofia and some of the Christians we had got to know in the institution. For some years, Ioan and Galina, Christians from the church in Sofia, had been visiting them and sharing the Gospel. We had met Ioan and Galina sometime previously at the institution, when we happened to be visiting at the same time. I can remember seeing Galina amongst the crowd of people listening to our message in one of the dark corridors indoors. It seemed to me that her face was shining and I knew instantly that she was the Lord's. Our meeting was another of the remarkable providences of God and we quickly became close friends and fellow labourers in the work. We discovered that Ioan had been abandoned by his parents himself and had grown up in institutions. Following his conversion, he had been given a burden to reach those still living in such places with the love of Christ and with the Gospel. Their lives were all out for God. Vanya, Larisa who was in her forties, Carolina and others had been converted through their testimony and had actually been baptised in the church in Sofia. This was one of the reasons which first drew us to the possibility of starting a second house in Sofia.

The owner of the property arrived and we all gathered into the entrance hall of the house to discuss our interest in purchasing the place. It all happened so quickly when I think about it. The owner was not drunk, but had obviously been drinking. After raising the price substantially above a price he had formerly named, he eventually conceded to the 15,599 euros we had originally agreed. We shook hands and left, having agreed to purchase the property. At the time we had all but a thousand euros of the sum needed, but we knew that this would use up all our available resources. We all posed for photos on the steps outside the front door, but those moments were also engraved on our memories. It was the end of a hot summer afternoon at the end of August 2008. A crowd of us had witnessed the proceedings and suddenly we were about to purchase a second house. There was a sense again of God's momentum about the chain of events and of being bystanders of His determination to deliver and to save. It was with a sense of wonder and great joy that we journeyed back to Chişinău that evening. For us it was the Lord's crowning blessing on a week labouring with joy alongside Him.

The name of the house was chosen during a car journey, when a member of the work team from Cardiff, named Matthew, was asked about the meaning of his name. He said it meant the "gift of God". We all agreed immediately that this perfectly described what we knew this new house to be—a gift of God—and the name was decided.

16

An Obstacle Course

With men this is impossible ...
(Matthew 19:26)

C asa Mea is the Moldovan registered charity which we set up prior to the opening of the first house. The text from the Bible which is enshrined in its constitution, and which acts as our watch-word, is Matthew 19:26: "With men this is impossible, but with God all things are possible." This verse became our reference point repeatedly over the next months. Our vision was utterly impossible from a human point of view.

When I was leaving Moldova at the beginning of September 2009 Liliana and I agreed that we would work towards 29th November of that year as the date for the opening service at Casa Matei. It was only three short months off, but we wanted to get the men out of the institution before the worst of the winter set in, if at all possible. I returned at the beginning of October.

To describe the situation we were confronting as "challenging" is a massive understatement. There was, firstly, the nightmarish bureaucracy within which we had to operate. It was necessary to negotiate an Everest of paperwork permission to start the second house. We became expert at tracking down ostensibly "lost" documents we had already submitted; obstructive, frequently rude officials became our daily testing ground; interminable hours were spent queuing in various Government departments to answer endless, often apparently pointless questions; and prevarication continued to the very last moment. The bureaucratic system that dominates is certainly not for the faint-hearted. Successful negotiation through such processes for an insignificant organisation like ours was, from the beginning, humanly speaking, impossible.

Logistically, there was no way we would be able to open the second house by the end of November. The purchase had yet to be finalised; the house, beautiful as it was, had no kitchen, bathroom or inside toilet and no running water; there was no access for people with disabilities—and at least two of the men we were considering used wheelchairs. We had no idea who would undertake the necessary work on the house, nor how we would find all the materials that would be needed. We were a long way from the land of B&Q and Yellow Pages! At the back of the house was a large plot of land that had been neglected for a very long time and was now jungle-like in appearance. The men about whom we were thinking all had high support needs and associated health problems—

much greater than the women in Casa Bucuriei—and there were no staff as yet and we were not sure how we would begin to find any. The village in which Casa Matei is situated is a long way from the city. Given the degree of stigma attached to people with disabilities, we were aware that the transfer of six men with problems from a closed institution to such a village would have been sufficient to provoke a local uprising in protest. The winter was fast approaching and its onset would make it impossible to undertake building work outside.

Added to this, the general context in which we were working was harsh. It often felt as though we were facing an ocean of physical, emotional and spiritual need and we would often ask the Lord, "Who is sufficient for these things?" (2 Corinthians 2:16) In the West we can be seduced almost into an anaesthetised sense of well-being. Although the same tragedies affect us from time to time, there are periods when our spirits can be dulled by the comforts of this life and the pleasures this world can afford. That is less the case in countries like Moldova. There is an awareness that death is real and that it is not only the elderly who die. There is harshness to everyday life and suffering is more evident. I seem to have been to lots of funerals in Romania and Moldova. There is an urgency to our work which is fuelled by the knowledge that heaven and hell are very real and time is short. There is a clear consciousness that we have to work whilst it is day. So the context is harsh, the needs, both spiritual and material, enormous and we, very few and fragile. An impossible scenario if one looks on a merely human level.

A further impossibility was perhaps the most serious. We

began to be aware that we were in the midst of a furious spiritual conflict which we could not possibly win with mere human weapons. The Government machinery began to crank into active mode about three weeks before the house was due to open. Interrogations, interviews and visits by Government officials began in earnest and the women in Casa Bucuriei became used to answering numerous questions about their attitude towards their current situation. There was a disarming and very convincing quality to the forthright answers they gave such officials— always to the effect that they were delighted with their new lives and would on no account want to return to the institution from which they hailed. On one occasion a group of four officials visited Casa Bucuriei and one had the sense that, although they were impressed by what they saw, there were strong, unspoken reservations.

That evening, an official we knew who was a Christian, and who had helped us a great deal in the past, phoned to warn us that she did not think our application to open a second house was going to be successful. It appeared that two people with positions of influence at Government level had petitioned the Government for permission to be withheld. They had argued that our only interest was to "change the religion" of those we supported and they had communicated many very damaging lies about us. There was no possibility for us to refute these things. My heart was grieved at the injustice of it all and our inability to respond with counter-arguments. I am a very slow learner in these matters. There had been previous occasions when I had been deeply affected by damage to personal reputation and had nursed those wounds for much too long. The Lord was teaching me that it was only His opinion that mattered at all and there was absolutely no point trying to defend such a nebulous entity as "reputation." My Moldovan friends knew immediately that our only possibility was to resort to prayer. My instinctive response was to fret and to try to think of some way of retaliating. It was, of course, futile to think along such lines and I realised that prayer was all that would effect any change. So we prayed to the God of heaven in our desperation and called on him to intervene against these seemingly impossible obstacles. We believed that He would deliver the men and that He would also redeem them.

A day arrived when one of the Government officials wanted us to take her to Casa Bucuriei, where she interviewed the six women about their experiences of living there, and to Casa Matei, which was still far from ready. She was an astute woman and dealt with us circumspectly but kindly. Having seen Casa Matei, and with the long day now far spent, she decided that she would like us to take her up to the institution at which the men were living, in order to interview them about what they wanted to do.

The journey was slow, over deeply rutted mud tracks, but we eventually arrived as the sky was beginning to darken and the temperature was dipping quickly. Given the important status of our passenger we were greeted with particular solicitude and attention by the Director and staff—an unusual experience for us. Tea was served in china cups and biscuits provided, which we devoured with great haste, having hardly eaten that day. The official visitor made it clear that she would like to speak to the men for whom we were requesting permission to move out to Casa Matei. There was a flurry of activity and the men were quickly summoned and brought. I can recall the scene so clearly! We had no idea how they would respond to such an auspicious meeting.

Slava and Petru arrived first. We could see them half-running towards the Director's building, faces etched with worry. Grişa wheeled himself in boldly to the Director's room and took up position opposite our friend from the Government. Vitali was carried in and placed on a wooden chair. Vanya was carried in like a sack of potatoes by another resident and dumped, lying sidewards, on two chairs because he is unable to support himself. We were much in prayer about the outcome. Gheorghe sat quietly observing the proceedings at the outset.

It was clear that the official was about to start questioning them, but without any of the direct eye contact or encouraging exchanges that would have helped the encounter. Before she could speak, Grişa burst out, "It's really horrible here. I want to go with them. When can I go?" He repeated these comments several times and this emboldened the others. Vanya, Petru and Slava indicated their desire to follow suit, whilst Vitali, when questioned, quietly and politely expressed his desire to remain in the institution. This saddened us greatly, but was no surprise as he had told us of this previously, fearing an unknown future and desperately afraid to lose the little help he currently received from other inmates there. Gheorghe spoke out vociferously about his wish to go to the house also, and as quickly as possible, and became very animated about the things he had had to suffer.

There was no denying the very clearly expressed wishes of the five men who wished to move. The official expressed her conviction that she had now heard with her own ears what the men wanted to do and that there was no dispute in this respect. They were asked to leave the Director's office and we spoke to them, explaining that we would visit them again that week-end. At this point Grişa became very distressed, saying that he could not stay there any longer and wanted to leave with us now. In an attempt to quieten him and get him out of his room the Director gave him his calendar, so that he could number the remaining days there and tick them off as they passed. This subdued him just a little, but he left the room shouting that he wanted to go to the house as soon as possible.

A long journey back to Chişinău followed, but we silently praised God for his interventions that day and for his great goodness to us. The official told us that we would receive her decision the next day. Late the following day Liliana phoned her and was told that she had spoken to the Government Minister himself, and that they had decided to give us permission to go ahead, initially for a three-month trial period to see how the men settled and how well we looked after them. How we rejoiced and thanked God! Hallelujahs ascended to heaven that day from our rejoicing hearts.

We believed that this last, great obstacle had successfully been cleared—as indeed it had—and that the way was now completely open to bring the men out in about ten days' time. We could see nothing that could possibly stand in the way. But we were forgetting that our spiritual enemy was strong and would be furious at the liberation of the men and at their coming under the sound of the Gospel and consistent Christian influences.

A few days later we made our way to the institution again.

We had meant to get there earlier in the day, but had been unavoidably delayed. By the time we were driving up the track towards the great concrete walls and metal gates it was already dark and snow was falling fast, casting a grey glow in the darkness. We hurried inside. Almost everybody was indoors and the corridors were swarming with figures wandering around in the semi–darkness. Hands reached out as usual to greet us and to seek our immediate attention. We made our way to each of the dormitories where the men who would move were living.

In the first of the very crowded dormitories we saw Petru sitting on his bed, looking very disconsolate. I asked him where Slava was—there was no sign of him and they were always together. He pointed under the bed vaguely. Thinking he had not understood what I was asking, I repeated the question. This time he again pointed under the bed, but this time in a more determined fashion. I knelt down on the dirty floor and peered under the bed. Slava was crouched in a corner under the mattress with a terrified expression on his face. As soon as he saw me he darted out from under the bed, rushed across the dormitory, and locked himself in the bathroom. On no account could he be persuaded to come out. A member of staff was sitting on a nearby bed grinning at the proceedings.

It became obvious that the large dormitory was full of turbulent disquiet. The staff members present were either taking great delight in the distress of the men who were designated to move to Casa Matei, or complaining loudly and bitterly. The reason for their complaint was the injustice of taking away some of the men who were their helpers. The reality was that the more able-bodied of those living there were constantly used by staff as unpaid carers. They did most of the heavy work and the jobs that the staff had no wish to do. Those living there who were very dependent on others for help with daily living tasks were usually helped by other inmates and not by the staff. Staff usually did the absolute minimum required and were often found asleep when they should have been working.

A very distressed Vanya explained to us that the staff had been cursing him from morning to night for moving. Gheorghe, who offered a tremendous amount of physical help to others at the institution, had been made to feel dreadful because he was considering leaving and staff would have to undertake the many tasks he had been doing. A member of staff screamed at us whilst we were talking to him, accusing us of removing her "right hand man." Gheorghe was clearly in a dilemma as to what he should do. Grişa wanted to get out of there as quickly as possible.

We eventually managed to extract Slava from the bathroom. In the most agitated fashion he spilled out a confusing story about not wanting to move on any account, because he had been told they would be used as slaves and would have to work very hard indeed all the time, and that they would be moved to an even worse place than the institution if they came with us. The staff and other inmates had deliberately fed him lies about the kind of place he was moving to and he had believed them. Perhaps saddest of all, we spoke to Vitali. He was sitting in his wheelchair slowly painting. It was almost impossible to get any response at all from him; he was very quiet and seemed most depressed. All we could gauge was that he did not want to move.

We left that afternoon with the distinct impression that,

with the probable exception of Grişa, nobody was prepared to move and that the whole development of Casa Matei had made things very much worse for the men. It seemed impossible now that they would ever agree to move the following week. As we left, the blizzard and the darkness set in. The weather seemed to reflect our situation. Driving back I had the sense that Satan was laughing at us. "How dare you assume that these men are yours? They are so afraid and confused now—they will never agree to go with you!"

We had, it was obvious, under-estimated our opponent.

17

Provision for Casa Matei

... but with God all things are possible
(Matthew 19:26)

Yet again our only resort was the Lord, and yet again
we cried out to Him who had "disarmed principalities
and powers" (Colossians 2:15) to help us. Only He was
able to deal with our strong enemy.

Encouragement came through the account of Gideon
in Judges 7. Gideon was faced with an impossible array
of enemies, Midianites and Amalekites by the thousand.
Fearful, insignificant and bereft of confidence, he was finally
persuaded to take up arms to lead the people into battle. The
Lord even allowed him to overhear the telling of a dream in
the Midian camp, announcing that the Lord had delivered
Midian and all the host into Gideon's hand, to show him that

the Lord would get Himself the victory. But in order that there should be no possibility of boasting that any human hand had obtained the conquest, the Lord depleted the army of warriors to a mere three hundred. So the Lord gained the battle with a tiny handful of Israelite soldiers against a vast host of the enemy, so that all would see that He had done it by His own right hand and so that no flesh could glory.

Such was our experience. There was not the slightest doubt that it was the Lord who overcame every difficulty and gained for Himself great glory in Moldova. It would have been laughable in the extreme to have even suggested that it was achieved by human interventions. Sometimes I have to pinch myself to realise that He has allowed me to see such things, but all the time a conviction that I was a mere observer of the wonderful works of God gripped and grounded me.

So how did He do it? The impossible bureaucratic mountains were, by some means, successfully negotiated. Even now I am not quite sure how, against all the odds and the fiercest opposition, the Government Minister gave us the go-ahead for Casa Matei. The Lord removed every single impediment even though we had been warned that this would be impossible.

Soon after we agreed to purchase the house, the Lord provided us with a team of very able workmen (and women!) Three men and a woman worked round the clock in all weathers to get the house ready. The bathroom was added on and eventually boasted a plentiful supply of hot water for the shower; the water supply was connected; the whole house and the small house at the entrance were painted from top to bottom and the broken windows replaced;

central heating was installed; a kitchen fitted; the jungle at the back was cut down and even ploughed before the onset of the worst of winter and a glorious view of the lake from the house came into view. A group of us from Chișinău would try to go up for one or two days each week to help with the work. A disabled access ramp was built up to the entrance of the house; some new windows and a new door fitted; piping was fitted underground and a new roof put on the extension that had been built. The house was transformed! But there was no furniture and we had no means of purchasing any—all our capital had been used up on the purchase of Casa Matei.

Some friends in Cardiff had, for many years, been running a charity called Support for Romania, which had made very many trips to and from to Romania to help with humanitarian aid. They had helped us also, but we had always had to find a means of transporting the goods over the border to Moldova from Romania, and this was by no means easy. We approached the head of Support for Romania, Alan Penrose, a man much used of God. He very kindly said that we could choose whatever goods would be of help to us in Casa Matei from their enormous warehouse and they would make arrangements to bring the things over in one of their lorries to Moldova. This was the Lord's amazing provision for us. However, the logistical difficulties of getting the goods into the country were only just beginning.

We had heard from many who had tried to get humanitarian aid into the country of the mountain of difficulties which needed to be overcome. Almost without exception those we spoke to had faced such insuperable obstacles that they had either abandoned the attempt half-way or had been stuck, literally for days at the border, only to fail in the attempt and leave with their goods undelivered and tempers frayed. Beginning to get the paperwork ready in Moldova, and starting our enquiries with the relevant Government Department, served to confirm what we had heard. Every single item coming into the country as humanitarian aid had to be described, enumerated, costed and weighed—including plastic cutlery! Photos were needed of all the items coming across the border. We were told that the Government would requisition at least 10 per cent of the goods for emergency purposes and that we would have to pay a fairly substantial sum for the work of the customs officials.

By some means all the paperwork was completed and permission granted just before the trucks were due to leave Cardiff. The two brothers driving the truck from Cardiff, Brian Topley and Alan Lewis, were also bringing required documentation with them. Our excitement mounted as we knew that they had left and were making the long overland journey from Cardiff to Moldova. It was October and the weather was unseasonably good. On the day appointed for their crossing, we made the long journey up to the border to await them. The Romanian customs were negotiated in about an hour and we received word that they were waiting on the Moldovan side. From the border fence we could see the lorry with Support for Romania written on the side. How our hearts praised God!

The customs official, after some prevarication, let me through as I had a UK passport. Liliana and Anea could not pass through with their Moldovan passports until much later, when a kindly official took pity on them. I located the lorry and knocked on the cabin door. Brian looked down and spotted me and he and Alan got out of the lorry for a joyful reunion. There was an awareness amongst us all that we were in the Lord's purposes and that He alone would see us through the seemingly impossible bureaucratic maze. A good friend from Romania had also come across to help with the whole process.

The lorry had arrived early afternoon on the Moldovan side. It was late at night by the time the contents had been sealed, the documentation stamped and approved and we were able to leave. The real customs check had yet to take place in Chișinău on the following day, but it was with great thanksgiving that we all drove down to the capital, leaving the lorry and its contents in the safe, guarded compound of one of the Russian churches in Chișinău. Having arrived at Anea's flat, we all squeezed round her small table and enjoyed food and fellowship with such thankful hearts.

The next day began early and Liliana and Alan took the lorry down to the customs post in the city. They were there for an extremely long, tiring day, but eventually all the paperwork was processed, the goods released without the necessity to forfeit 10 per cent to the Government, and we were in possession of a lorry full of goods intended to furnish Casa Matei. We parked outside Casa Bucuriei that night and by the time we arrived back there early on Saturday morning kind friends had already unloaded the goods intended for Casa Bucuriei and we were able to start out for northern Moldova. It was a beautifully sunny day.

Help was on hand again when we arrived at Casa Matei and all the furniture was unloaded quickly and stored in the house. An older sister from the church, Sora Lidia, had invited us all to lunch—she is a near neighbour of Casa Matei. A huge amount of food was perched precariously on a very small table, around which we squeezed. Our mealtime was interspersed with prayers of thanksgiving and prayer for the salvation of her unconverted husband. It was a precious time of fellowship. The afternoon was now far spent and we needed to leave. We drove before the lorry up to the Romanian border crossing and left Brian and Alan in "no man's land" where we waited until we were sure that they had crossed successfully.

18

Soviet Days

... a famine ... of hearing the words of the Lord
(Amos 8:11)

Whilst we were waiting for our friends to depart I had the opportunity to survey our immediate surroundings. I had a real sense of "deja vu." The former vestiges of Soviet Communist border controls still remained, although now virtually unused. The tall, dark watchtower, now empty, was visible in sharp relief on the horizon. A sentry guard box was positioned to our right, at the approach to a narrow strip of road leading to the main crossing point. Alongside us, stretching away into the distance was the old, tall fence marking the border, topped with now rusty barbed wire.

We waited there for what must have been a couple of

hours. The night was falling and a chill, harsh wind was blowing, which froze our faces. From time to time we spotted off-duty border guards cycling nonchalantly across a field between us and the crossing on what looked like very old bicycles. They lit a fire to keep warm and collected pieces of fallen wood to fuel it. There was an almost light-hearted atmosphere to their comings and goings. It was in stark contrast to scenes that flooded into my memory from former border crossings, many years previously.

With others, I had been involved for a number of years in taking Christian literature into communist Eastern Europe during the 1970s and 1980s, before the Berlin Wall fell. From soon after my conversion the Lord had placed on my heart and mind an inescapable burden for His work in Eastern Europe. This quickly led to visits to many of those countries and growing friendships with a number of the Lord's people we met there. They were days in which we witnessed something of the oppression Christians were enduring in those times, their thirst for the Word of God, and brightness of the image of Christ in so many of their lives.

But the border crossings had always to be faced before it was possible for those meetings to take place and the literature delivered. They were tense times. Leaving with a large vehicle from the UK or Europe, the beginning of the journey was always pleasurable, crossing country after country in Western Europe and always looking forward to the time when Southern Germany was reached and the grandeur of the Alps began to come into view. What a glorious sight that was!

Austria having been reached, with its pristine orderliness and colour, our apprehensions would begin to rise. The impossibility of the task we were facing would dawn again upon our consciousness and the consequences of being discovered with our load began to take on fearful proportions. Our only resort was prayer and our only deliverer was the Lord Himself. Many people were involved in such ministry in those days—there was nothing remarkable about our own participation. But it was a very good training ground.

Having left the poorer outskirts of Vienna we would often make our first entrance into Eastern Europe via Hungary. There was a marked contrast between the affluence and vibrant colour of the Western Europe we were leaving and the dull drabness of Eastern Europe and its sense of strange oppression. That was true even of Hungary, which was then one of the less obviously oppressive countries. The approach to countries like East Germany or Czechoslovakia took on more fearful proportions. It seemed that we always had to cross an ostensibly endless neutral zone before reaching the formidable border crossing points. Sometimes we would try to arrive during the night, knowing that fewer border guards would be on duty then. But whether it was day or night there was a palpable tension as the vehicle drew up beside the guards and they climbed into the vehicle whilst we got down. Hearts and unspoken prayers would cry out to the Lord to help us. There were some near-discoveries. Once, at the crossing into East Germany, which was known to be particularly fearsome, a border guard, who was clearly suspicious about our vehicle and its possible contents, told us to drive over to a part of the border territory apart from other vehicles whilst he tracked down some tools to dismantle the inside panels of the van. He was angry and accusatory. We waited there a very long time for him to return—he had taken all our papers with him. Silently we prayed, but began to envisage a not altogether pleasant outcome. Finally he returned. It appeared that he had been diverted by some other urgent business. He had no time to detain us further in order to conduct a more extensive search of the vehicle and, in some obvious frustration, he handed us our papers back and told us to leave. Our thanksgiving to God may well be imagined!

Once into a country the pressures did not disappear. There was always an awareness that known association with us, as Westerners, could bring national Christians into danger with the authorities, so we took pains to visit them often at night and to park a long way from what we believed to be their address. Simply locating an address was frequently problematic in the absence of published maps or clear street signs, and asking for directions was not an option.

But they were days in which we experienced the quite remarkable intervention of God to help us on a number of occasions. For some years we followed up Christian radio contacts in a country to which friends of ours regularly broadcast the Gospel on the radio. The family we were seeking, the Polohas, were close relatives of the Christian radio broadcasters we knew. Their situation was hazardous as they had relatives who had left the country without official permission. It would have been extremely unwise to have drawn any attention to our quest. I remember that we drew into a parking place near the centre of town wondering whatever we should do. Almost unobtrusively a man, and someone who looked like his daughter, walked up to the open window of our vehicle. He whispered the name of the family for whom we were seeking in a questioning way. We could not believe our ears and our delight at finding those for whom we had been seeking so long was impossible to disguise. He quickly indicated that we should follow their car and, keeping a considerable distance between us, we eventually arrived near their home, to our great rejoicing.

On another occasion we had returned, exhausted, from a busy visit to an Eastern European country and had arrived in Vienna, anxious to find the camp site and rest. We drove through the city for what seemed like an interminable time, hunting for what appeared to be a non-existent camp site. It seemed beyond belief that in such an organised, well-directed city we found it impossible to locate such an obvious place. As we reached some traffic lights a vehicle drew up alongside us and the driver shouted up to me from her driving seat. She said in perfect English, "Follow me to the camp site!" Having thus communicated she drove in front of us until we reached the camp site, when she left us. There was no simple human explanation for the occurrence and I was convinced that we had had an encounter with one of God's ministering spirits "sent forth to minister for those who will inherit salvation" (Hebrews 1:14)."

Such memories were re-kindled by the sight of the long miles of border fence which we saw again at the Moldovan crossing. I was reminded of a conversation I had had with a Slovak pastor as we looked at similar fencing from inside his country many years previously. We talked about the visible signs of being shut off and locked into their communist political system. He spoke of his sense of spiritual freedom in the Lord Jesus Christ, despite the presence of such external oppression. He said that his spirit could still fly like a bird.

There were many memories of men and women I had met over the years, whose hearts burned for the Lord Jesus and whose love infused their actions. In those days it could be very costly to indicate that they had anything to do with Westerners, let alone greet them warmly in a public place. But I remember, in Bratislava, Czechoslovakia, one older brother, who had been to prison for the Gospel, ignoring all the dangers inherent in his actions and embracing us most warmly in a place where he could be seen by others. Many Christians would understandably have been afraid to do this, but his fearless, loving gesture imprinted itself on my mind. Some of those brothers and sisters are safe home in glory now and that brother is amongst them. The Lord will have owned his courage in showing us the love of Christ in such circumstances, "for which reason He is not ashamed to call them brethren" (Hebrews 2:11)."

On one occasion a fairly large quantity of Christian literature we were carrying in our vehicle was discovered by border guards at a crossing into Czechoslovakia. It could have been very much worse. The literature was confiscated and our passports received a *persona non grata* stamp, which meant that we were not allowed back into that country for five years. This was a cause of real grief, as it meant that we would be unable to visit those Christians there who had become our great friends. On this occasion we had brought some written addresses of Christians with us. Usually we would never have done this, recognising that the implications for those people were dangerous if the addresses were found, but some friends we had met en route had persuaded us to take these with us. There were too many to memorise, and so we were detained.

I asked to go to the toilet in the middle of the questioning, recalling that I had the addresses and realising I needed to destroy them. Having closed the toilet door, I began to tear up the paper with the addresses on, in order to flush them down the toilet. As I started to do this the door was pushed open very roughly and the remaining papers snatched out of my hand. Someone had clearly been looking through the adjoining wall of the toilet. I was ordered out and asked to strip by a female border guard. In those days I was very thin and we joked subsequently about the authorities using photos of me to prove how malnourished Westerners were! We were kept there for most of the day and, after more questioning, finally allowed to leave towards evening, minus our precious cargo. It was with heavy hearts we made the journey back across no man's land again, much more quickly than we had anticipated returning.

The Soviet Union had always been my first love in terms of spiritual burden. On an early visit to that vast country with a group of youth workers I remember walking across Red Square late one night on my own. In those days the gleam of the huge red star over the Kremlin stood out, in contrast with the darkly macabre spectre of Lenin's mausoleum. But I was overjoyed to be there, in this country over which my soul yearned. I sang the words of one of my favourite hymns as I walked across the cobbled square: "We have heard the joyful news, Jesus saves!"

19

Casa Matei Begins

God has chosen the weak things of the world to put to
shame the things which are mighty
(1 Corinthians 1:27)

Just one day remained before the opening service that had been planned for Casa Matei. The six men who had been given permission by the Government to move out of the institution into the house had not been allowed to visit Casa Matei previously and today was the day when they were to move in. One can imagine a little of the bravery it necessitated on their part to make such a move into a completely unknown situation. Despite knowing us, and hearing descriptions of the house and the possibilities of a new life there, it was nonetheless a tremendous step for them to take.

We had been up late at night before getting the house ready for their arrival. Curtains were being hung not long before midnight and finishing touches to the bedrooms made. The day dawned full of anticipation for us. I had stayed behind at Casa Matei with some others whilst a group took a minibus to bring the men out. How we prayed as we did some of the final cleaning and waited! There was no means of knowing whether the men would agree to go with those who had gone to fetch them, or not.

What actually happened on the group's arrival at the institution was disturbing. Staff, still resenting the possibility of losing some of their helpers, had continued to fill the men's heads with tales of how horrific life would be if they did decide to go. They would be "used as slaves" and they would be left without any means of support at all. They would be in great danger if they decided to leave. By the time our friends arrived the men were frightened out of their wits! One of them, Vitali, had already decided that he would definitely not move. Vanya and the others would go only on condition that, if they did not like it there, they were free to return to the institution. Late that morning I received a text to say that the helpers and five men were on their way to Casa Matei. Apparently two of the men, Petru and Slava, both of whom have Down's syndrome, had tried to visualise the way that the minibus was taking so that they could get themselves back if they decided they did not want to stay!

The moment of their arrival is imprinted on my memory for all time. The minibus drew up outside the gates and the men got out. Their clothing was poor and they each carried a sack full of their meagre clothes and possessions. They gazed in an awed way around them and responded to the love of those who had accompanied them and who now welcomed them to their new home. Smiles began to appear, together with the most enormous sense of relief on their part. Tentatively they entered Casa Matei and curiously examined items of furniture, cupboards and beds. We had our first meal together, all gathered around the tables in our big kitchen, which had been rapidly assembled only the day before. The good food was devoured with much pleasure. They were used to eating as quickly as possible before the food disappeared or was stolen, so we gently encouraged them not to make unnecessary haste. It was also previously their custom to brush any crumbs or remaining scraps onto the floor and after that first meal we found the carpet in some state of disarray.

Following the meal, it was time for the men to choose new items of clothing they would like to have. This was such an enjoyable task for all concerned. We had been given a large amount of clothing by churches in Wales and it was like going to a men's outfitters for a new set of clothes. Showers and baths followed, together with hair washing and shaving at a leisurely pace. They had not had the opportunity to wash properly for a considerable period of time and all relished this opportunity. Vanya, who needs assistance in every aspect of daily living, so enjoyed being partially submerged in warm, soapy water and then wrapped in clean towels that he asked how often he could expect to receive such a wonderful experience. His body was covered in sores from lack of proper attention, but these disappeared after some days. The wood stove was lit in the evening and the house became pleasurably warm. The men looked with a mixture of disbelief and delight at their clean bedding and their pleasantly furnished rooms. We prayed together and retired early, knowing that the next day, when the opening service was due to be held, would be a very full one. With great thanksgiving we drifted off into sleep.

Very early the next morning found all the helpers awake and already at work. It was a cold, grey day. The outside of the house was festooned with balloons and ribbons and friends from faraway Chişinău began to arrive early. Amongst these were the six women from Casa Bucuriei and Sora Angela and Sora Galina, members of staff there. They greeted the men with kindness and then sped round the house comparing notes with Casa Bucuriei and concluding that they much preferred Casa Bucuriei!

By mid-morning the house was full and there were also neighbours listening from the street outside, where we had set up a microphone. True to Moldovan culture, gifted singers had arrived from the capital and the house was filled with wonderful music, with the volume very loud. The men were dressed in their best outfits and entered in fully to the proceedings. The service opened with the cutting of the ribbon by the local mayor and Wyn Hughes, the pastor from our church in Cardiff. Prayer followed from leaders of local churches and our pastor. As is customary in Moldova, arms were raised in fervent prayers of blessing on the part of the pastors. A glance to the left of them revealed Gheorghe, one of the men who had moved into Casa Matei the previous day, with his arms also raised similarly in blessing. Those of us who saw him took great joy in this seemingly confused gesture on his part.

Preaching of the Gospel followed, with many eagerly listening. The man from whom we had purchased the house, together with a number of neighbours, seemed to drink in these most wonderful truths. It was a day of very great rejoicing. Late that night we returned to Chișinău, our minds filled with memories of the last days' events. At the same time we were very conscious that we were leaving five men, who had only just left decades of institutional life, in the hands of two new members of staff who barely knew them and who had little experience in the work. How would things transpire? We need not have worried. The God who had brought all these things into being was to take care of the following days and months in His own miraculous way.

When I visited soon afterwards Sora Olga, one of the members of staff, said to me, "I so love coming to work. It does not seem like work at all for me—it is a place I look forward to coming to very much." The staff were very hard-working and they taught the men to take part in the household chores and in the upkeep of the ground and the care of the poultry. It was with a real sense of pleasure and growing self-respect that the men learnt practical tasks such as using the washing machine and the gas cooker, preparing food for meals and keeping the house clean and tidy.

I remember visiting during early July of the following year. The house had only been open for about seven months. Waking early I went into the back garden. It was a most beautiful summer morning. The sound of flocks of birds could be heard from the lake at the bottom of the garden and the water was shimmering in the early morning heat. There was a stillness everywhere. I could hardly believe my eyes as I looked upon the garden. In every direction, as far as the eye could see, there was a harvest of fruit and vegetables. Ripening tomatoes, peppers, maize, onions, herbs of various kinds, potatoes, cucumbers, vines beginning to hang with small green grapes, apple, apricot and nut trees beginning to display their fruit—it was a veritable Eden. Later on that summer, having bottled and preserved and eaten as much as we possibly could, we still had a surplus, to the extent that we were giving away tomatoes and grapes. How we praised the God of heaven and earth who had so bountifully provided for our physical needs! "You crown the year with Your goodness; and Your paths drip with abundance" (Psalm 65:11).

The bounty we experienced was not only on a physical level. From the beginning we had longed that the men who moved into Casa Matei would be saved. We were very conscious of the need to provide a better situation for their temporal needs, but it was for their eternal salvation that we longed above all else and we prayed towards this end. At the time of the move only one of the men, Vanya, was clearly the Lord's. Not all the men have good verbal ability and three of them have moderate learning disabilities. They are all illiterate. As we got to know them better it was important to see from their behaviour if there were any changes that would indicate a work of grace beginning in their hearts. All of the men are such characters and it was not difficult in the slightest to become genuinely fond of them and to try to show something of the Lord's love for them.

Gheorghe is in his forties and is the physically strongest of the men. The staff in the institution had particularly not wanted to lose him and he had been used as a modern day slave there, being called upon incessantly to undertake the heaviest manual work. His speech is indistinct until you get to know how he tries to communicate; he laughs loudly and often and is very expressive. One of his hands is semi-paralysed. He eats with great gusto. We were anxious not to abuse his willingness to help, but discovered soon that he loved to work in the garden and to chop logs for the wood-burning stove. Later on he became responsible for looking after Casa Matei's cow. With great pride and attention he takes the cow up to pasture each morning and returns with her each evening. On arrival at Casa Matei a great bear hug from Gheorghe is the invariable welcome, together with a face beaming with smiles. There was an early awareness of an interest in spiritual things on Gheorghe's part, going back to the time when we knew him before the move. He always enjoyed the services we held in the institution and would come daily to listen to messages at the camp we held, always bringing others with him. At Casa Matei it was very evident that he really enjoyed attending and participating in the church services and in the informal times of worship which were held in the house.

One day, not long after the men had moved in, the Director of the institution they had left and several of the medical staff made an unannounced visit to the house. The visit seemed to go very well and they appeared pleased with how the men had settled and with the conditions in the house. They stood up to leave and were heading towards the door when Gheorghe grabbed hold of the Director's coat, obviously wanting to retain him for some purpose. Closing his eyes, and folding his hands in an attitude of prayer, Gheorghe proceeded to pray. Much of what he said was indistinguishable, but we recognised phrases such as "bless the Director," "help the men in the institution," and "thank you." After some minutes, during which time the

Director and the medical staff had respectfully bowed their heads also, Gheorghe finished praying with a fervent "Amen" and a beaming smile. It had been the most sincere gesture on Gheorghe's part and was characteristic of his belief that prayer was very important.

On another occasion we took Gheorghe to see his mother—they had not had any contact for about forty years. As part of our work with the men and the women we set about searching for their long-lost family members. It was important for them to have some sense of their family origins and we also explored the possibility of renewing contacts if there was sufficient interest. Without exception, none of the family members with whom we made contact wanted to receive their relative back but a small number were interested in renewing contact. The reception we received was very variable.

On the journey to Gheorghe's home in a village he reminisced about his childhood memories of his mother and their house. We arrived to find a well-kept and well-furnished house and a substantial plot of land behind the house. Awaiting us were his mother, who was now in her seventies, and a number of nephews and nieces in their teens or twenties. His mother smelt strongly of alcohol but greeted Gheorghe warmly and with some apparent pride in her son. The nieces and nephews, conversely, visibly backed away from him and were embarrassed and uncomfortable by his presence. With understandable curiosity Gheorghe looked around the house from which he had been taken decades previously. He is not prone to crying, but at one point he sat down on a bed and wept as though his heart would break. I thought it very possible that this was because he had some comprehension of his family's potential ability to have cared for him all those years ago—but instead he had been rejected and forgotten. He quickly regained his composure and chatted amiably with his mother, putting his strong and caring arm around her diminutive frame. We persuaded her to return with us and Gheorghe for a few days to Casa Matei, for her to see where her son was living. She agreed and the next few days found them together at Casa Matei. Often Gheorghe could be heard telling her it was much better to pray than to get drunk and that she should ask God for help.

And so we observed how, quietly but persistently and in many other ways, what we believed to be a genuine work of grace was wrought in Gheorghe's life and heart. It was very clear that he loved the Lord and had a hunger for spiritual things and a practical love for those around him.

Slava is in his thirties and has Down's syndrome. He loves to chat and he loves to look at books, even though he cannot understand the contents. Very quickly adjusting to his new life at Casa Matei, despite his initial fears, he has become a hard-working and much appreciated member of the home. During the first weeks after his move there items would frequently go missing, only eventually to be discovered in Slava's chest of drawers. This was a habit he had acquired in the preceding decade. Often there was something almost amusing about how he would take a bottle of shampoo from someone else's cupboard and, very obviously to everybody else, deposit it among his own belongings. But clearly it was not the kind of behaviour we wanted to encourage. A member of staff discovered that the only influence which would have any effect upon such behaviour was if she read to Slava Bible passages that instructed against doing such things. This would have an immediate effect on him. He listened with great attention and would change his behaviour as a consequence. The Word was actively working in his life.

None of the men had ever been on holiday. During their first spring at Casa Matei we had arranged for them to attend a Christian camp for people with disabilities, run by Brother Dima. The week before saw each of them busily making preparations for their time away. They were due to leave at 2pm on a Saturday afternoon. At 5am that morning there was a tapping on the window of our bedroom. We looked out to see each of the men already dressed in their finest attire and with bags packed! A large supply of patience on their part was needed to wait until their departure much later that day.

That year they attended two camps, each lasting a week. The locations were very pleasant—wood cabins canopied by tall trees providing gentle shade from the hot sunshine. The camp programme was invariably busy each day and the men entered in readily and enthusiastically to whatever was happening. There were lots of messages from the Bible, mostly given by Brother Dima. Learning new Christian songs played an important part in the programme and the men chose to stay up until late each night to sing and to listen to the beautiful music of a balalaika orchestra or a group of singers who had come from the capital. There were testimonies from individuals attending the camp and games and competitions as well as simple drama presentations of stories from the Bible, in which they took part. They and the staff who accompanied them had a most blessed time and nobody wanted to leave at the end of the camps. Returning home, Slava told everybody that he had been "to heaven, to Jesus' house." Later on that summer Slava, pointing to himself, told me quietly "Jesus in my heart." There was a reality about his faith that struck everybody.

And so this God, who had so powerfully delivered them from so desperate a place, showed Himself powerful also to redeem them. His everlasting love for them, conceived in eternity, began to be revealed in time.

20

A Hidden Work of the Spirit

... the secret place of the Most High
(Psalm 91:1)

Our second camp at the institution in the north was drawing to a close. The formal part of the programme had ended and I was looking for individuals to speak to who had remained behind. It was a hot, sunny day and under the shade of one of the big trees I saw a woman sitting in a wheelchair away from the rest of the crowd. She greeted me with a gentle smile and in answer to my questions explained that her name was Sasha and she was forty-three years old. Sasha was quietly spoken and showed that she was glad to talk with someone. It was clear that she was intellectually able, but her legs were contorted underneath her and unable to support her body, and her arms and hands similarly lay in useless, disfigured fashion on her lap. She probably had cerebral palsy, but in the absence of any physiotherapy her limbs had become locked in distorted spasm. Sasha explained that she was dependent on others to help her.

She began to tell her story and I listened with amazement. Formerly she had lived in the institution for women and girls from which the women at Casa Bucuriei were drawn. She told me that she had been converted there. On a later occasion she told me the story of her conversion. There had been a Christian member of staff who used to tell the girls Bible stories. Sasha said she so loved to listen and she knew these stories were true and she believed in the God of whom they spoke. One night she had a dream. She saw a very bright light and heard a voice saying, "You will not walk in this life, but you will run to Me." I did not remember seeing her ever before. Some years previously she had been transferred to this adult institution and had lived there ever since. I asked how she coped with living there, and said that I found the noise levels alone difficult to deal with, even during our short visits. Replying, she described how, when she needed peace, she would close her eyes and talk to her heavenly Father. She would try to dissuade those who shared her large dormitory from doing things that would displease Him. And then she said, with much animation, "But I will soon be at the feet of the Lord Jesus in heaven—very soon I will see him!" Our discussion showed me clearly that Sasha had a very real relationship with the Lord Jesus Christ and that she was eagerly anticipating the coming glory. I had a sense that the Lord was doing a work in these closed places which will only be fully understood in eternity. It seemed that sometimes men and women were being drawn to Him without any apparent human agency. And, once drawn by this all-powerful love, they were being kept, against all odds, until the day of salvation. I have often reflected that it is relatively easy to go into such closed places for a day and then to retreat to the normality of our own lives, and have wondered how ever I would survive if I were living permanently in such a context with no hope of ever being able to leave. Only a divine keeping would make endurance possible in such circumstances. There was an unseen King who was both saving and keeping His own children.

On a subsequent visit, not long afterwards, I sought out Sasha. I found her in a cold room with many other women. She recognized me immediately and smiled with pleasure at having a visitor—such a rare event for those who lived there. The other women in her room were sitting passively in rows on benches, many staring blankly and some rocking to and fro. As usual they were wearing their outdoor clothes in an attempt to keep warm. There was an unpleasant smell of damp and dirty clothes despite the chilling atmosphere. The television was blaring out in the background with nobody listening to it. I knew one of the occupants of the room well. Her name was Nadia and she had recently run away from the institution. By way of punishment she had been ordered not to go out of the dormitory for a month. She sat angrily and disconsolately on one of the benches, covered in cuts and bruises, glowering and periodically screaming abuse at anyone in her vicinity. There was a single member of staff who greeted me politely enough, but then proceeded to speak to other women in the room using the most dreadful language and threats—the kind of language that would only be used in the most punitive of places. A woman lying in a bed nearby called to me and I went over to see her. The bedding was both thin and filthy. The woman told me that she had not slept at all that night as she had had some teeth pulled out the previous day and could not sleep for the pain. Her face was very badly swollen. Nobody showed the slightest interest in her. Such was the context in which I found Sasha. It was a scene of dreadful cruelty, neglect and chaos. That was the situation in which she was being kept, with her eyes on the Lord. When she discovered that we were about to hold a service on a nearby corridor she eagerly expressed her desire to attend. I could see her throughout the short service we held, her face beaming with delight, joining in the singing of hymns and songs which she seemed partially to know. That morning I spoke on the verse "The blood of Jesus Christ His Son cleanses us from all sin" (1 John 1:7). She listened attentively.

The next winter Sasha became very ill. When I visited her I was shocked by her appearance. Her skin was drawn gauntly across her face, with deep hollows for her eye sockets, and she seemed to be so very thin. Her energy had disappeared and she preferred to spend time resting in bed, but when we were there she would always make a supreme effort to get up and come to listen to the singing and message. She never lost her big smile or her capacity for thankfulness to God for His mercies. Sasha often spoke of her longing to be in heaven—heaven was an ever-present reality for her. At one time she confided to me that even if there were another house she would choose to remain where she was. She said to me perceptively that it was very good that we came to visit her and others who lived there, but we came and went and her institution needed people who would stay there and tell others about the Lord Jesus. The cost of such service in such a place was for her personally enormous and it was a cost I would have shrunk from. The Lord knew all about her sacrifice and a crown of gold awaits her.

Early on in the work there we thought we had identified those who seemed to have a real faith, and there were about seven such people living there. As time went on, and we developed stronger relationships with many there and got to know quite a number, we realised that we had underestimated the number of those who were truly the Lord's. Sasha was one such example for us. It is a cause of continuing wonder to us that the Lord Himself has not forgotten those who live in such places and is doing a most remarkable work of saving grace amongst them.

Larisa was a young woman in her thirties whom I loved dearly. She and her father, Domnul Grişa, used to come to all the services we held. Although Larisa was not converted, she always loved attending these impromptu services. She knew all the hymns we would sing and would join in with great delight. She and her father were both blind. Larisa knew how to find her way round the institution by feeling the walls, although her mobility was poor and she sometimes fell and hurt herself. She looked after her father, who used a wheelchair, and she lived in a men's dormitory in order to care for him, which was a dangerous place for her. Their lives, from a human perspective, were full of deprivation and suffering. On one occasion Larisa complained of bad pains in her foot and leg. Her shoes were always old and broken and sometimes she wore men's shoes that did not fit her, or even two left shoes. We made a mental note to try to find some shoes that would fit her.

Some scenes remain imprinted on my memory. One summer day Larisa was washing some of her father's clothes with a rough bar of soap in an old metal pail outside in the hot sunshine. She asked for my help in arranging them on the outside stair banister so that they would dry. The water she was using to wash them was cold and very dirty and the trousers had not been rinsed properly, though of course Larisa could see none of this. Her concern was simply to ensure that her father had some clean clothing. After I had arranged the trousers over the banister a member of staff, unaware of my presence, came towards Larisa screaming the most terrible abuse. She quickly passed on her way but Larisa dropped to her knees and was left sobbing on the floor and inconsolable. I was distressed beyond words to observe all this and felt a determination, I think God-given, to do all within my power to take Larisa out of the situation in which she was currently living. The verse in the Scriptures which reminds us that we should do good to all men, especially to those who are of the household of faith, impressed itself on my mind and heart again.

Grigoriu, like so many others there, had very little occupation in the day-time and would sit endlessly in his wheelchair without any activity. Whenever we would visit, and tell him who we were, his whole face would light up and he would say, "The peace of the Lord be with you."

The second camp at this same place was most blessed. I had been full of apprehension when leaving with six others from my home church in Cardiff during the very early hours of one August morning in 2009. The father of one of the young people who was going had said to me shortly before our departure, "You will bring her back safely, won't you?" He was a missionary and he knew as well as I did that it was only the Lord who could guarantee her safe return. But my anxiety levels soared as the sense of responsibility for those accompanying me was reinforced. An arduous, white-knuckle ride in a Moldovan mini-bus from Romania to Moldova did little to help. The driver received a hefty fine for violation of virtually every traffic regulation at one point from the Romanian police, but subsequently continued to drive in exactly the same totally reckless fashion for the rest of the journey. In order to get more paying passengers, an extra seat had been added to the inside of the mini-bus in very make-shift fashion. When the driver made a particularly maniacal turn that seat became dislodged from its moorings and the occupant, one of the young people coming to the camp, was left clinging with all his might to the seat next to him to avoid imminent disaster. It was only with reluctance, and after driving some distance further, that the driver could be persuaded to stop the vehicle to attend to the dislodged seat. Hardly auspicious beginnings and it was with considerable thanksgiving that we eventually arrived safely at our destination.

Our days were full of activity. Prior to the camp, for example, one group had the unenviable task of constructing a duck pen at Casa Matei with little in the way of raw materials or tools. The ducks, which had previously been crammed into a small, dark, pen, benefited quickly from the *de luxe* accommodation that resulted from these efforts, and filled the air with quacks of approval.

One morning before the camp, a friend and I took the

men from Casa Matei for a walk round the village. The
day was splendidly warm and the walk was delightful. The
two of us pushed wheelchairs whilst the other three men
walked leisurely alongside. We walked all around the lake
in the village and passed geese, usually annoyed at our
approach, swallows dipping low over the water of the lake,
turkeys bustling out of our way, goats and cows, which were
invariably tethered to a stake of sorts. Passers-by greeted
us politely and we sat in the shade of some trees to enjoy
such lovely surroundings. I decided to hold a very simple
impromptu Bible lesson by the side of the lake. "Who is Jesus
Christ? What has He done? What happened after He died?"
The men joined in enthusiastically. I could see that Vanya
had a very clear understanding of these things and that
Slava was constantly affirming his trust in the Saviour.

Three of the young men who were to help with the camp
were sleeping in the outhouse to Casa Matei. It was their
first night there and late at night Carwyn, one of the young
people from Cardiff, thought he heard someone enter the
room—the outside door was not locked. He froze for several
moments in terror until he gathered sufficient courage to
awaken the other young man in the bed next to his. "Aled,
I think there's someone in the room," he whispered. More
frozen silence followed as the intruder proceeded to shuffle
nearer to their beds. Aled found a torch which he suddenly
shone in the intruder's face. The face of the third occupant of
their room, Bahktiar, a Kirghiz man, was illuminated in the
darkness. Uncontrollable laughter and great relief followed!

And so we made our way to camp. Our multi-national
team gelled quickly, despite language barriers. Potential
frustrations and stresses at the camp that followed were

numerous, but the tangible love that characterised the behaviour of those beloved Romanian and Russian-speaking brothers and sisters with whom we were working won over everybody. We experienced the joy of Psalm 133:1: "Behold, how good and how pleasant it is for brethren to dwell together in unity!"

For all of us there was something incomparably blessed about sharing the Gospel with those who lacked every human comfort and security. The evenings, too, remained in our memories. We would sit in the warm night beneath a sky studded with more stars than we had dreamt existed, singing the praises of Him who died for us and looking for the sure hope of heaven. Moldovan hymns contain a great treasure trove of praise, often born out of persecution and suffering and certain knowledge of the Lord's presence through it all. I believe that the effort of learning the language would be amply repaid by the resulting access gained to such wonderful hymns.

One such hymn, I was told, was often sung by Christians when brothers were being taken to prison for their faith in former days. A rough translation will communicate something of its beauty:

We are going with boldness to our heavenly country. We are following Jesus with joy. We are weak, but all our trust is in Him. He will keep us faithful unto death.

CHORUS: Joyfully with Jesus we go forward, we are following the Lord Jesus to our country above.

We have good news, news of forgiveness and we will spread
this news throughout the whole world. Workers are few, the
harvest is great, but we will bring many sheaves with us.

This world persecutes us. It persecuted Jesus too. A heavenly
crown is being made ready for us. By His grace we will be
strong in faith until the end.

That wonderful, great and awesome day is near. It will not
delay. We know that we will see Christ in greatest glory when
He comes for us.

Moldovan Christians love to sing—but it is not for the sake
of singing alone. Their hymns have the potential to take you
directly into the presence of the Saviour and to give you a
sight of heaven.

Our camp, that second year, was situated in a most
beautiful location. We were high up on a hill overlooking a
lake and surrounding fields. In the early mornings the red
sun rose directly before us as the mist lifted from the lake
and birds flew high in the sky. Storks landed early to forage
in the ploughed field behind us.

When we returned to Casa Matei, the men were
expectantly waiting for us, sitting in the sunshine outside.
Beaming, Vanya told me that he been praying for us all week.

21

Transformed Lives

... that they may have life, and that they
may have it more abundantly
(John 10:10)

When Anişoara first arrived in Casa Bucuriei, she was very withdrawn. She would rarely engage in eye contact with anyone and replied to anyone outside her immediate friendship circle with indistinct monosyllables. There was no doubt, however, that her trust in the Lord was strong. She used to speak in whispers to Diana, her closest friend. Fearful of strangers, particularly men, she would quickly disappear at their arrival. Very hard-working, and unfailingly helpful to others, she offered Diana very consistent support and help. The skills of housework, at first new to her, were quickly learned and she began to take a very active part in household tasks such as washing up and preparing meals. She has great energy and tends to run everywhere. Anişoara was more reluctant to venture out, apart from to church, being scared of the traffic and of meeting new people.

The Anişoara whom we now know has altered almost beyond recognition. She could not be described as pretty, but there is an inner beauty about the work the Lord has done in her life that shines. It is her love for Christ that most strongly characterises her. Of all the women in Casa Bucuriei, I would say that she is spiritually the strongest. Her favourite occupation is to talk about Jesus. Whilst unable to read, she has learnt much of the Scriptures through Christian radio and from church. Her first purchase with money she had saved was a radio and cassette player, bought to enable her and the others to listen to the broadcasts from Christian radio and her growing collection of Christian cassettes.

Anişoara is of diminutive build and has straight dark hair. She looks considerably younger than her thirty plus years. Her eyesight is very poor and her life has been very hard. Rejected by her family at a very young age, she spent her childhood and youth in one institution after another. Years of neglect caused serious health problems and at one stage, she later confided to us, she had eaten very little over a longish period as she had such bad stomach pains every time she ate anything. As a child she had experienced repeated abuse at the hands of various staff members. She began to be terrified of men. It is no wonder that she came to us with so many fears and was so withdrawn in every way.

As with other women, we attempted to make contact

with her long-lost relatives. The search proved much more difficult in her case. The address of somebody who could possibly have been her mother was eventually given to us by a town hall in a remote village. When we visited the address in question, the woman inside refused to answer the door after hearing what our quest was about. She shouted abusively through the closed door, "I don't know you and I don't want to know you!" We left our contact details with a neighbour but heard nothing else from her again. It seemed to us that there was quite a possibility that this could have been Anişoara 's mother. Having received this information, Anişoara responded with amazing serenity. "Maybe I don't have anybody here on earth, but I have the Lord." She would repeat this fairly often and with complete peace and without any sign of envy of some of the other women who had occasional contact with formerly long lost relatives. Here was grace indeed.

One evening when I was having supper with the women in Casa Bucuriei, Anişoara, smiling, began to talk about the verse in the Bible where it says that the Lord does not look on the outward appearance but on the heart (1 Samuel 16:7). Her joy in the Lord's love for her was obvious. She takes great delight in listening to the Word, in praying and singing the Lord's praises. Despite a speech impediment she will eagerly speak of Him to anyone who is willing to listen. She has remarkable ability to care for others in the most practical of ways and will quietly and unobtrusively demonstrate the love of Christ in action. Now, far from disappearing to avoid contact with you, Anişoara will eagerly seek friendship and fellowship. Her eye contact with others is much better and she is glad to talk these days. It is as if her whole being has flourished since the move to Casa Bucuriei. She and the other women often talk about the Lord's intervention in their lives and their life before the move and afterwards. They attribute what has happened only to the love and power of God at work in their lives—and so do we.

Diana is in her twenties and uses a wheelchair. She is not in robust health and has had several periods of hospitalisation for various ailments. (During one of these times I was very concerned to see hospital staff using the same needle for different patients using a drip. The incidence of hepatitis B and C is high and I wondered to what extent it was attributable to the re-use of needles in medical settings.) Although the youngest of the women in Casa Bucuriei, Diana has sometimes become their informal leader. Strong-spirited and determined, she will frequently see what needs to be done in the house and make sure that someone attends to the task in hand. Converted at her former institution through Anişoara, she was drawn powerfully to the Saviour and knew that her life had changed for ever. And how this Saviour kept and cared for her!

Diana's mother had told her long ago that she had been born with a disability because her mother's boyfriend was a violent man who had kicked her repeatedly in the stomach when she was pregnant. We had no means of knowing for certain whether this was true, but we thought it likely. All the women began to talk about their childhood memories the more we got to know them and the safer they felt in their new environment and Diana was no exception. She related how she and her mother had spent years begging on the streets of Moscow and other cities in the most terrible cold and deprivation. Often they were forced to sleep on the streets, such was their poverty.

We eventually managed to trace Diana's mother and took Diana to visit her. She was a youngish woman but prematurely aged by her hard life. Work was hard to find, but when she was able she would spend long hours labouring in the nearby vineyards. When we first visited her with Diana she was living in a village in a poor house which was owned by others. It is typical of Moldovan hospitality that the very best of food will be provided for visitors. Despite their obvious poverty, the most lavish meal began to appear on the table. Diana was clearly delighted that her mother had gone to such trouble. There was a new boyfriend on the scene who showed not the slightest interest in Diana throughout our long visit. Other distant relatives and neighbours began to appear later that day, curious to see this long lost daughter who was disabled, but they engaged in very little direct communication with Diana; she was more an object of novelty value than a person visiting her home for the first time in many years.

Following that first visit Diana's mother continued to contact her from time to time and even to visit when she was motivated sufficiently to spend money on the bus fare. On one occasion, when Diana was in hospital, she agreed to stay with her for a few days—it is important for patients to have a carer in hospitals in Moldova. However, it was clear both to us and to Diana that her mother had other priorities in life than this, her only daughter. Diana was thankful for those times when her mother did contact her. She had not the slightest trace of bitterness against her and prayed for her regularly. In all this we saw the fruits of the Spirit manifest in Diana's life. One evening I was staying at Casa Bucuriei overnight and Diana came into my room to talk. She will often do this late in the evening and we have had many precious times of fellowship and sharing on such occasions. As I became increasingly sleepy, she gave me a big hug and said, "I love you very much and I pray for you every day."

How my life has been blessed by these women! I am upheld by their prayers and greatly encouraged by their faith and lives and their close walk with the Saviour. A godly contentment and thankfulness characterises their behaviour. For a number of years I have had little in the way of natural family and it often feels unusual not to have the support of a family, which most people experience. However, despite this lack, I embrace the words in Mark: "So Jesus answered and said, 'Assuredly, I say to you, there is no one who has left house or brothers or sisters or father or mother or wife or children or lands, for My sake and the gospel's, who shall not receive a hundredfold now in this time— houses and brothers and sisters and mothers and children and lands, with persecutions—and in the age to come, eternal life'" (Mark 10:29–30).

The Lord Himself has given me brothers and sisters and mothers and children I could never have dreamed of. Through them he has crowned my life with loving kindness and tender mercies. No soul that is drawn out after him and who takes up His cross and follows Him will be without his reward. The Lord will choose blessings for that person in great abundance and in ways that one could scarcely have believed possible.

22

Our Needs Met

"... did you lack anything?" So they said, "Nothing."
(Luke 22:35)

As the work grew, the responsibility we had taken on often weighed on me heavily. Sometimes, particularly in the middle of the night, I would recall that we had taken on lifetime responsibility for seventeen adults with disabilities and I would worry about the future and how we could possibly continue to meet those responsibilities. A third house, Casa Alex, had now opened. All sorts of concerns would come flooding into my mind, especially when my thinking dwelt on the three of us who were involved. I was getting older and who knew how much longer I would have sufficient health and strength to remain involved? Anea was working all the hours there were and frequently had episodes of ill-health, partly because she pushed herself too much. Life expectancy in Moldova was not long and I had known so many who had died at a relatively young age. Liliana would probably marry one day and would no longer have time to remain as involved in the work as she had been before. The future for the work looked precarious.

Added to this, I was aware of a number of enterprises in Moldova that had begun with great enthusiasm, and sometimes with considerable resources, but which had eventually folded. I had contact with some of them started by those who were not Christians, where initially great changes for good had occurred, but then the workers had wearied of the corruption and bureaucratic impediments with which they were surrounded and had given up. They had left very disillusioned, disappointed and sceptical in the extreme about the possibility of making any real impact in Moldova.

Over time, a number of people we had relied on as seemingly indispensable helpers in our work emigrated. We grieved over their loss and wondered how we would be able to continue without them. Veronica, who had first introduced me to Moldova, had left with her parents for America, where she had married and settled. I could hardly imagine how we could continue without her. Olga had married and settled in Spain, where her husband had found work. Tragically her young husband was killed in a building accident soon after the birth of their daughter and Olga was left widowed in her twenties. Ioan and Galina, who had been so pivotal in the work in the institution, had also decided to emigrate to the States with their children. Again and again we seemed to lose key labourers in the work. It was necessary constantly to remind ourselves that it was the Lord who had brought the work into being, and that He would see it through and meet our needs. The danger was always that if we looked to ourselves we would despair of our frailty and transience. However, our expectation was in Him; we would not be disappointed.

From the beginning prayer has been the cornerstone of our work. Early on I was approached by brothers and sisters from my home church in Cardiff who wanted to start a prayer group for the work of Casa Mea. It happened almost effortlessly, but that group have followed the work with detailed and faithful interest and there is not the slightest doubt that God's blessing and protection have followed us as a consequence of their persistence in prayer. A wide age group is represented amongst them. Some of the older members, although never having visited Moldova, pray for individuals there with an earnest and informed interest. They have rejoiced with us and they have shared our sorrows. I am absolutely certain that the Lord raised up this group of prayer supporters and it is He who has given us this indispensable foundation for the work. So Jehovah-jireh began to provide. It was their practice to meet for prayer together on the third Thursday of every month. Soon we began to meet at roughly the same time in Moldova on the same evening to pray for those in Cardiff and for the work here.

But how ever were we going to provide for the growing financial needs of the work? It has been our practice generally not to request financial help for the work but to pray that our needs will be met, believing that "God's work done in God's way will never lack God's supplies." Such a method seems almost quaint in today's context of maximum exposure of needs to as many people as possible, using the most sophisticated technology available and the most skilful fund-raising expertise. Our needs were considerable—the funds needed for the purchase and adaptation of three houses with land; furnishing of the houses; the costs of registering our charity in Moldova; the responsibility for feeding and clothing seventeen adults for the rest of their lives; medical costs (all those we support have serious health problems of one kind or another); salaries for the staff who work in the houses; the costs of summer camps; purchasing and maintaining the transport needed; hire of larger means of transport when required; the cost of petrol ... The list of needs was seemingly endless and with time became longer and longer.

It was clear to us very early on, that we needed to become increasingly independent of income from the West. With that in view, we did all within our means to make the work as self-sufficient as possible financially and, after a long struggle, we managed to get the Government to agree to hand over the pensions of those we were supporting, together with some rights to reductions in gas, water and electricity costs. The land around the houses was productively used for food and by each winter fruit and vegetables in abundance had been bottled and stored. Pigs, goats, poultry, rabbits and a cow were kept for food. The women in Casa Bucuriei learnt how to produce high quality goods for sale in the UK and in Moldova, from which they received a small income. They and the men in Casa Matei learnt how to economise and to understand the value of money. The annual costs of each house were progressively reduced by such means. But there was still a considerable financial gap that remained and we did not have the means to supply that need.

Careful financial accounts have been kept since the beginning of the work. It is our testimony that we have lacked for nothing. Somehow every single need has been met, and that often abundantly. Sometimes individuals not directly connected with the work in any way have given large gifts totally unexpectedly. A couple in the church at home were celebrating a special wedding anniversary. They decided that instead of presents, they would like gifts to be given towards the purchase of a much- needed vehicle for our work in Moldova. Together with other contributions we were soon able to purchase a second-hand minibus from Germany and bring it to Moldova for fitting. It has seven seats, space for a wheelchair and much room for luggage and has been invaluable in our work. I have previously spoken of our indebtedness to an organisation called Support for Romania which often rallied to our assistance and over the years has transported a treasure trove of goods to Moldova from the UK, including furniture, clothes, and disability aids. How generously the Lord has met this need!

Each time I returned to the UK there were speaking engagements and the number of those interested in and supporting the work in which we were involved gradually grew. This was all of the Lord's doing. Sometimes, despite my nerves about speaking publicly, there were meetings when we had a sense that the Lord Himself had drawn near. Such occasions always took me by surprise and I marvelled at the kindness of God in visiting us with His presence.

Liliana, Anea and I often reflected that it was only the Lord who could have raised up such a groundswell of support for us and for the work. When we looked back to consider, time and time again, how the Lord had brought us together at first, and subsequently begun to show us what great things He could do, our hearts filled with praise. Only He could have so gloriously woven together such a chain of events and have raised up such an army of believers with a heart for the work. We noticed that our growing number of visitors left spiritually affected for good by their visit, with a sense often of profound blessing and of having met with God in a fresh way. Such was the Lord's plan to encompass others in the circle of those touched by the power of His work in Moldova.

As time went by Anea continued to work at the factory but, with increasing regularity, her health began to suffer as she continually tried to work twelve-hour shifts and also make herself available to the growing demands of Casa Mea, particularly once Casa Alex opened. It began to be obvious to us that this could not continue and I began to think about the possibility of Anea joining us full-time in the work of Casa Mea. With work in such short supply in a country like Moldova it would be considered foolish in the extreme to give up a job—and Anea had a good job as head of the section where she worked. It was a massive step to think about and once we began to talk about it her mind was assailed by a torrent of worries about how ever she would survive without the seeming security of paid employment at the factory. She told me that the enemy of our souls seemed determined not to give her any peace if she should take such a step. However, the Lord spoke to her and she knew that she had heard His call and she decided that she would willingly and with all her heart obey Him and trust Him for the consequences. She arranged a meeting with the Director of her factory to tell him the news. He was furious (probably at the thought that he was going to lose one of his best workers) and shouted at her that if she ever needed work in the future she should not come begging to him. The Director reminded her of the implications of giving up a good job and the medical care that went with it. Anea cried to the Lord that she would have no regrets at all at her decision and would not look back once she left. The peace of God flooded her mind and soul after making this decision and God confirmed its rightness to her many times through his Word. How we praised the Lord! We knew that she would be of great blessing to us full-time in the work and to many whom we supported. We realised that we would be able to reach very many more people than we had previously. Anea dreamt that she saw the women of the southern institution standing at a window waiting for her to visit them. We had to trust the Lord that she would not lack any good thing and that she would have the means with which to live.

In November 2011 we celebrated the fifth year of Casa Bucuriei. We chose to have a thanksgiving service in the church in which the six women were members and it proved to be another evening of great blessing. Local dignitaries had been invited and we were thrilled to see the local mayor, doctor and nurses from the local clinic and the social worker from the village. They all expressed their pleasure at the fact that Casa Bucuriei was situated in their village. The women from the house sang and testified to God's faithfulness over the preceding five years and the Gospel was preached clearly to all who were present. I knew that the Lord had allowed me to see "the goodness of the Lord in the land of the living" (Psalm 27:13) and my heart rejoiced. We had not lacked any good thing. God had been faithful in every respect.

23

News of an Awakening

That He might make His mighty power known
(Psalm 106:8)

Word began to reach us of a great awakening that was occurring in a Gypsy community just over the border from Moldova, in Romania. Before long we were hearing songs from this revival on Christian radio in Moldova. The women from Casa Bucuriei quickly learnt them all by heart and would play them at great volume when they were broadcast on the radio. I too came to love both the words and the melodies whilst I still knew little about the setting from which they derived. Here were Christian songs full of the message of Calvary and of a Saviour so powerful that He could wash the worst sinner and set him on the road to heaven. We rejoiced to hear them.

I was already aware of the sizeable Gypsy communities of Romania in Oradea, the city where I had lived. Little by little I had learnt more of what God was doing amongst this community of Gypsies. It seemed that one man from their large village had been working in Germany for a long time. By his own admission he had been up to no good there and, although he had become prosperous, it was by means of which he was subsequently ashamed. It was in Germany that he heard the Gospel and was saved. From this time the Lord so worked in his life that he felt a compulsion to return to his own village in Romania to tell his fellow Gypsies about this Saviour who had so remarkably changed his life. This call proved irresistible and he went back and began to search for Christians amongst his own large community.

He found a tiny handful of discouraged believers who were meeting in the kitchen of someone's home, sharing a few verses of Scripture and praying and singing without anyone to lead them or to preach to them. He, who was without any previous theological training, but who was on fire for the Lord, began to preach every evening. He said that his first pulpit was a kitchen table. To his own acknowledged surprise others began to join them in these small kitchen meetings and Gypsies began to repent and be converted. It was not long before the kitchen was too small for their gathering and they had to move to a large garage where he continued to preach and where many more were brought under conviction of sin and saved. It seems that even though the conditions in which they met were most uncomfortable—there was no heating in the depths of winter and usually only standing room—nothing could stop men and women from coming to hear the Gospel preached and nothing could stop an increasing tide of those newly confessing the Saviour.

The garage quickly became too small for their meetings and they began to build a large church. Most of them were very poor indeed and they prayed for the materials they needed for the construction work and these were provided in the most unusual ways and to the thanksgiving and encouragement of all. Over the last few years many hundreds have been saved and baptised. In two years nearly a thousand Gypsies from this area were baptised. Baptisms usually took place in a river with hundreds taking part. The recordings of these baptisms are like scenes from the New Testament.

The young church faced severe persecution. Those opposed to the work would enter their meetings and threaten them with knives or pistols. Some notorious previous criminals became Christians. One of them had been regarded with terror by the whole Gypsy community. He used regularly to steal from them and if he entered a house the occupants would automatically give him what he was demanding in the knowledge that if they refused to do so they would at best be beaten up and at worst killed. This man, once converted, was himself beaten up several times and, to the amazement of his attackers, did not respond in kind. He is now one of the leaders in the church. This kind of transformation was repeated in the lives of many. The local police and local government officials have frequently remarked on the incredibly decreased number of difficulties they are experiencing from this former problematic community. The new church building is now filled to overflowing—there are normally about 3500 in the services—and they are already seriously considering the need for a larger church that could accommodate five thousand. The work of deep repentance and faith continues.

My first contact with Roma communities of any size had been in Romania, as in Oradea, where I lived, there had been a large number of Gypsies. I quickly became aware from my students and Romanian friends that there was a deep-seated antagonism towards Gypsies and a general unwillingness to associate with them—they lived in separate communities which had little to do with the general population. I also became aware that there was a kind of "under-class" in the Gypsy community that gained a reputation for abandoning their children in the maternity hospital soon after birth and seemed to survive on the proceeds of stealing and begging. I met a resistance from most students when it came to working with Gypsies. This was by no means total resistance thankfully, but was of sufficient strength for me to have to deal with it from time to time. With this in mind I was obviously intrigued by what I was hearing. The brother whom God used at the beginning of the revival in Romania felt the rejection of his people strongly and often remarked that the Lord had chosen a small despised people to visit with extraordinary power and grace.

It has been a revival of such proportions that news of what was happening rapidly reached us in Moldova. Eventually some of the members of the new church were persuaded to visit Moldova both to preach and to sing. On one of those occasions they had been invited to take part in a tent mission organised by one of the large Pentecostal churches in Chişinău. The women from Casa Bucuriei and I were very keen to attend and one warm evening in May we piled

into our newly acquired minibus and drove over to the tent
mission site. We managed to secure seats inside the tent,
but by the time the meeting began at 6pm. all the seats
inside the enormous marquee had been filled and the side
flaps of the tent had been rolled up to allow those standing
outside to participate. There was row upon row of people
standing outside for the entire service.

The service went on until about 10pm, and none of us
wanted to leave even then. After prayer and a great deal of
wonderful singing, a Pentecostal pastor from Bucharest
preached. All the proceedings were seriously loud; this is
often characteristic of Moldovan services and is in stark
cultural contrast to the usually more subdued services in
the UK. Although I would not by natural preference choose
such loud music and such loud preaching, I have become
accustomed to it over the years and it does not distract me
as it did initially. Whilst we were singing and listening to the
preaching, which alone continued for about two hours, we
became very aware of the Lord's presence amongst us. The
Lord Jesus revealed Himself through the Word and we had a
glimpse of His majesty and mighty sacrifice and His love for
sinners. It was most wonderful. Although I was only dimly
aware of what was happening around me, so compelling
was the sight of the Saviour, I realised that there were men
and women around me crying out to God both with praise
and with cries for mercy for their sins. A deep conviction of
sin felt by all of us led to a glorious sight of a Saviour who
calls not the righteous but sinners to repentance. It was
unforgettable. It was as if we had shared a small part of
the experience of awakening that had touched the village
where our Gypsy brothers and sisters lived. A large number

of Gypsies living in Moldova also attended services such as these and were greatly blessed and encouraged.

There is no doubt that the Holy Spirit brings the Word with great conviction to souls in revival. This has been my personal experience and my observation of what has been happening in Moldova. There is no escaping the all-seeing eye of the Holy Spirit. He exposes sin, past and present, to our view, and the soul shrinks from the just judgement of God and the knowledge that hell is real and a place where our sins will undoubtedly take us. A holy fear of our great God overcomes the soul. Preachers will bring such realities awesomely before our view, and the wretchedness of our state and our sense of disgrace before such a God come with great clarity. Then Christ will be brought before us gloriously, and His triumphant work on the Cross, and the soul will flee to Him for cleansing and forgiveness. It is a most powerful work and it leads to deep repentance and the salvation of many.

Here are a people who are eagerly looking for and expecting the second coming of the Lord Jesus Christ. They are watching and waiting for Him to be revealed on the clouds of glory. This seems to mark one of the key differences between Christians in Moldova and those at home. It was brought home to me through one particular incident. At one stage both Liliana and Anea were able to visit the UK. The time was most blessed, but just as they were leaving Anea asked me what I thought was a most telling question, "Are the brothers and sisters here looking for His appearing?"

I have listened to many preachers both in Romania and Moldova who preach with a fearlessness to take your breath away. They have had an unforgettable encounter with the God with whom we have to do, and His fear has possessed their souls. Fear of man has evaporated. John Knox , the sixteenth-century Scottish Reformer, once said, "A certain reverential fear of my God who has called me ... to whom I knew I must render an account when I shall appear before his tribunal ... had such a powerful effect as to make me utter so intrepidly whatever the Lord put into my mouth, without any respect of person." A consequence is that the congregation is confronted with eternal realities in a way that is totally compelling and denies the possibility of escape from such truths. The Lord makes such men into preachers who are mighty in the Word, and it has been my great privilege to listen to the preaching of these spiritual giants.

Liviu Olah, the former pastor of the Second Baptist church in Oradea, and the men who were with him when the revival broke out, took a daring stand in most dangerous days for the Gospel. He refused to compromise with sin and was known to be a man of prayer as well as a preacher powerfully used of God. Men and women would arrive at church at 7am on Sundays to be much in prayer before the service. In a recording I heard from 1974 he preached against the weak, formalistic repentance that was present in so many churches in Romania at that time. Although many attended church, he pointed out that the difference between the lives of believers and non-believers was not as marked as it should have been. "People are dead in their sins and heading for hell and we need to be on our knees and crying out to God for their salvation! If we are not completely at His disposal men and women will go to hell! If we believed how dangerous their state is we would be completely consecrated to God ... We are guilty as Christians. We have been indifferent to Christ but Christ was not indifferent to our state—He died for us—so great was God's love for us ... You will perish without Christ! Don't delay! Without Christ you are eternally lost and going to hell ... May those who are called the repentant ones be brought to repentance." He told those who were about to be baptised not to do so unless they were willing to give themselves wholly to the Saviour at any cost.

Those present remember that at this point the power of God fell on the congregation and believers and unbelievers alike could not but cry out to God for mercy, such was the overwhelming sense of their own sin. Men and women in the vast congregation knelt and cried out loudly to God. There was much weeping as God poured out His Spirit on this congregation and filled His people with a passion for prayer and for spreading the Gospel and for living a holy life. It had a remarkable effect on that whole city.

Pastor Olah's declarations during the revival reveal his burden: "It is not enough to see our sin—we need to see Christ!" "Don't forget that hidden sins in God's people prevent blessing just as much as open sins." "Delay is the most subtle weapon of Satan with regard to salvation." "Revival delays because there is too little and too superficial prayer from God's people." In his book, *Marea Importanţă a Rugăciunii* (The Great Importance of Prayer), Olah writes (author's translation),

I received a deep inner conviction to pray for the conversion of a multitude of souls. This was in the spring of 1965. Parallel with this was an inner revelation that there would be a very great revival in Romania which would be the means of vast numbers turning to Christ. I remember praying for our country that God would bless it with an unforgettable outpouring of grace and that the Word would be preached on the radio, on television, in the stadiums, in public squares, in newspapers, magazines and in books ... I want to say something about the prayer group for sisters from the Second Baptist Church in Oradea ... I want to thank God for the work of about fifty sisters who fasted and prayed intensively for the work of God. I am convinced that God used this group of sisters very especially in the outpouring of great grace on this church. About a year after I became pastor of this church, I went into the room where these sisters were deep in prayer—they were not aware of my presence. They were so involved in prayer that not one of them looked towards me. There and then I said to myself, 'This prayer group is the reason for the hundreds of people that have been converted in the last months!'

A "Chance" Encounter

He who opens and no one shuts
(Revelation 3:7)

November 2010 had been unusually warm. In Moldova we were used to the first snows early in the month. It was already mid-November and we were still enjoying gloriously warm, sunny days. When we visited churches in the villages Christians were praising God for such warmth because they could not afford the cost of wood that was used for heating. The sunsets were glorious. Wide vistas stretched before us when we were away from Chişinău in the evenings—hill after hill rolled away in the distance, becoming ever more misty; the deepest pinks in the skies would be reflected on the surface of numerous lakes in a beautiful cascade of colour and late in the evening such lakes would be full of fish busily creating rippling circles on the surface of the water; avenues of trees, high like vaults above us seemed to protect our way as we sped through; fields ploughed ready for the spring with dark, rich earth prepared for the deep frosts that would follow; peaked haystacks punctuating the scenery here and there; workers labouring in silhouette against the setting sun; women with headscarves knotted under the chin. Then the light disappeared completely. One of my abiding memories is of wintry sunsets—a muted pink fan of light right across the horizon reflected in the dulled sparkle of the lying snow. But this was different. Here was weather with an almost summer feel.

One Friday morning during this most beautiful November we were making the long journey to Cahul in the south of Moldova to meet with Brother Dima and to deliver many things for people with disabilities that we had received from Support for Romania. It was a clear, sunny day and our journey took us past the very gates of the institution from which the women in Casa Bucuriei had come and from which we had been barred for a number of years. Long before arriving there it was possible to view the three main blocks of the institution near the top of a hill from a considerable distance and on this particular morning they came into view very early. With what memories that sight filled us! As we got nearer we began to wonder if we would be able to see some of the women we knew over the gates as we passed. And so we drove slowly up the big hill to the place itself and began to peer eagerly out of the window of the vehicle. What happened next was a miracle.

As we approached the buildings we became aware that

there was a large group of women working outside the gates with some of their staff—I think they were clearing up fallen autumn leaves. We could not believe our eyes. Encouraging the drivers to pull up, we scrambled down from the vehicles, straining to see if we knew any of the women outside. As we did so a shout went up from the women who had been at work and, arms waving and faces smiling, they all rushed towards us and we quickly found ourselves being tightly embraced by very many who were calling out our names and trying to get themselves heard in the general melée.

They had so many questions! Not least were many questions about whether they could move into one of our houses and if we would be building more. Many hailed us with the traditional greeting used between Christians, "The peace of the Lord be with you." There were requests for prayers and for Christian music and messages. It is hard to explain how indescribably blessed we felt to be in their company again. We were overwhelmed by the Lord's kindness in allowing us this totally unexpected opportunity to see many of them again. I became aware that years had passed since we had first come to know these women and both they and we had grown older. There was a sense that these had been akin to "wasted years" for many of them, having only experienced the restricted life of an institution. I longed that they should know something different.

During the general uproar and gladness, we became aware that the Director of the institution, who had commanded us so forcefully not to have any further contact with the women, was herself driving a mini-bus out of the gates. One of the staff indicated to us that we should beware as she could see us. Being alerted to this, Liliana quickly ran over to her to explain that we were simply on our way to Cahul and had seen the women and could not but greet them. Instead of responding, as we anticipated, with rancour, she smiled and said that we could enter the institution itself if we wanted to and we could bring the women from Casa Bucuriei along to visit their friends if we arranged a suitable time with her. Liliana explained that unfortunately we could not stop for very long at that time as we were expected in Cahul, but that we would love to make a visit in the future.

Making our farewells to the women we returned to the cars to ponder on God's intervention that morning. It was as if He had stretched out a finger and so arranged the whole order of events that we should reach the institution at the very time when we would be able to see and speak with the women and also the Director. What amazing love and care! Once again we had not the slightest doubt of our God's glorious sovereignty in all things and His delight to bless His children with the most wonderful surprises of His own right hand. We meditated much on the events of that day.

Four months later found us back at the institution. We had spoken to the Director on the phone and she had agreed to us making a formal visit again this time into the institution itself. She received us most warmly in her office and Vera and Aliona, who had come with us from Casa Bucuriei, presented her with a bunch of flowers and some chocolates. Only three days previously, she explained, she had been discharged from hospital—we were aware that she had ongoing health problems having contracted Hepatitis B and Hepatitis C some time previously. There was a deep scar on her neck which we had not seen before, indicating some kind of surgery.

The Director told us that she had given up the idea of building ten houses in the grounds of the institution in which to house and train some of the older women. Our idea of having ordinary houses integrated in the community was the better one, she told us, and that was what she hoped would develop in the future. We had not expected such a radical change of viewpoint on her part. She added that she thought institutions like hers should be restricted only to those in severest need and numbers should be limited to a hundred or so. She went on to speak more personally about the fragility of life and shared with us that her sister-in-law, who was fifty-three, had terminal cancer. We shared with her that there was a woman in our church who had her photo on her bedside table and prayed for her every day. With this her eyes filled with tears and she thanked us. Anea spoke of God's love for her.

We were invited to a birthday celebration which followed; it was a communal event to congratulate all those who had had birthdays during that winter and we were pleased to be invited. There was much singing and competitions, accompanied by shrieks of laughter, but it was all very institutional, with almost no individual attention. Afterwards the Director said that we were free to spend time again in the institution and it was with much joy that we walked round, greeting many that we had not seen for some time. How very kind of the Lord to allow us that opportunity again! How very characteristic of His goodness to be working in the heart of the Director whilst we had been away! Many spoke to us of the Lord. There were some blessed reunions, and how my heart ached for these women!

One of them said to me before we left, "He is preparing a big place for us up there in heaven."

I noticed that the situation of those who were immobile had only marginally improved. In various rooms they were lying listlessly on bean-bags and there was a dreadful smell in such rooms. Staff were in evidence, but largely inactive and indifferent. It was bitterly cold outside when we reluctantly left eventually. I reflected again that God is no man's debtor. We need to await His time to act and we will see His power then. The psalmist's words are as relevant today as when first written, "Be still, and know that I am God; I will be exalted among the nations, I will be exalted in the earth!" (Psalm 46:10).

25

The Third House—Casa Alex

Even ... shall ... the prey of the terrible be delivered
(Isaiah 49:25)

By the beginning of 2011 we were becoming more distressed by what we were seeing during our visits to the other institution in the north. That winter was particularly cold and it seemed that Siberian blast after blast found its way to Moldova and we froze for months on end. There were incidents at the institution which we could not erase from our thoughts. One Saturday morning three people died there, none of them particularly old. The complacency with which their departure was regarded affected us deeply. Not infrequently we discovered a large number of people locked all day in a room which was devoid of furniture with the exception of benches and perhaps one or two bare tables. Anea, with her usual determination, would insist that one of the workers, albeit grudgingly, unlock the room and we would enter, usually to discover a number of women poorly clad and cold, many rocking to and fro and some clearly mentally ill. As the door opened those inside would all swarm towards us desperately seeking some kind of human contact and activity.

One day I went into a room and discovered Jura, a man we had got to know quite well and who had shown real interest in spiritual things. His state was truly pitiable— his clothing was filthy and he was in a world of his own. He was muttering to himself, seemingly oblivious to his surroundings. All the other men in his room were in a similar state of total neglect and each had a far-away look of profound sadness. There were no staff to be seen.

One of the young women we knew died soon afterwards. She was thirty-one years old and her name was Raia. For years she had been looked after by one of the Christians living at the institution, Carolina. Raia could do nothing for herself. All day she would lie on a bed with her head hanging down backwards from the bed. She would have to be fed in this position and, in the most sacrificial yet unobserved way possible, Carolina devoted herself to caring for Raia. Afterwards we reflected on the fact that although Carolina's years of service for her dependent friend had passed with no outward recognition, there had been One who had observed everything and who would not forget what had happened. Without Carolina Raia would have died much more prematurely. However, one day Raia's stomach started to swell and she began to be in great pain. Nothing was done to alleviate her situation medically until it was very late indeed, when at last she was transferred to the hospital in Soroca. Carolina went with her—it is expected in Moldova that patients will have a carer if needed. It was too late to save Raia's life and she died in the hospital. Nobody told Carolina what had happened for some days and the news came as a very great shock to her when she was eventually told and returned to the institution. She felt completely bereft.

Visiting soon afterwards we were able to speak with Carolina about what had happened and her great grief. Another young man, Simeon, who had also been a great friend of Raia's, was badly affected by losing his friend in such tragic circumstances. We found him sitting under his bed listening to Christian radio for some comfort. Simeon has cerebral palsy and is in his thirties. He uses a wheelchair and is most often to be seen sitting outside on his own with his poor clothing soiled by food stains. It would be very easy to pass him by with very little attention. However, time spent engaging him in conversation reveals a most profound understanding of the Gospel on his part. I have often wondered, listening to him struggling to articulate words, how the Holy Spirit revealed to him such a depth of understanding of the grace of the Lord Jesus Christ and the way to heaven when his life has been so very constrained on every hand. Such is the wonderful work of the Spirit, who reveals spiritual treasures to the children of the Most High God. I remembered again God's promise to me many years ago, "I will give you the treasures of darkness and hidden riches of secret places" (Isaiah 45:3).

As individuals in a team, Liliana, Anea and I can operate very differently. In spite of this, by God's grace alone, we have known over the years the most blessed unity and love for each other. Anea and I both tend to be impulsive and plunge into action and consider the consequences only afterwards. In God's goodness Liliana is the exact opposite to this and provides a very thoughtful, reflective, prudent, considered counter-balance to our impulsiveness. A result of this combination is that if we are all agreed on an important action we can be fairly certain it is from the Lord. Such was the case with the third house. By January 2011 each of us was so affected by things we had seen at the institution over the preceding months that we knew that we had to act. It was a God-given confluence of opinion. When Anea and I heard Liliana saying that we needed to think urgently about a third house we could only agree with all our hearts. What happened subsequently revealed to us again the sheer speed with which God can act when he chooses—indeed He rides on the wings of the wind.

In an incredible way we found ourselves in possession of sufficient funds to consider buying another property. Although we had no idea how we were going to fund the running-costs of three houses and support the needs of seventeen people with disabilities long term, we reasoned that if God had given us enough for the capital costs we could trust him for the rest.

Another house in the village of Sofia came naturally to our minds. Two of the women we were considering bringing out of the institution had had links in the past with the church in Sofia and they knew some of the congregation. We agreed that we would not have more than two houses in any one village to avoid the possibility of creating any kind of ghetto for people with disabilities. But we thought that two houses within easy reach of each other would not be problematic and that optimal integration in the village and church would still be possible. So we began our quest for a house with some of the Christians in the local church advising us on potential properties which were for sale.

The search was not a long one. Having viewed some houses (including one very dilapidated dwelling where the very elderly inhabitant offered us her free services as a trained nurse!) we asked to view what was subsequently known as Casa Alex. The house had been repossessed by the bank as the owner had got into debt whilst trying to finish the construction work there. However, it was he who showed us round first in February 2011. The house was not very much more than a solid concrete shell, with building work only half completed in most rooms. But we could see its potential. It stood in an attractive and substantial plot of land with a well and possessed the all-important Moldovan cellar in which to keep produce over winter. There was a pleasing arched entrance to the main door and sufficient rooms to accommodate all our needs. In addition there were some wood-burning stoves which heated some of the walls, which would present us with some real economies in heating costs. Most of the windows looked out pleasantly onto the garden outside and were light and cheerful.

After discussion and prayer Liliana made the owner an offer which he promptly refused. Both Anea and I were inclined to offer more but Liliana was sure of her ground and stuck to the original offer. Every time we saw the house we longed for it to be used for the Lord and to become a house of great blessing for those from the institution. We prayed that it would be ours, much as Caleb had prayed,

"Give me this mountain" (Joshua 14:12). Some weeks later we returned from church on a Sunday evening and Liliana received a phone call from the owner of the property saying that he would accept the original offer. We whooped with joy and knelt to thank God with all our hearts. We read Psalm 118:15–16, "The voice of rejoicing and salvation is in the tents of the righteous; the right hand of the Lord does valiantly". Our friends in the UK shared our joy.

The house needed very considerable work to make it habitable and we wanted to move the people from the institution in as soon as possible so that they would not have to spend another winter there. During one of our visits to view the house, John Mark Teeuwen from the Unevangelised Fields Mission was visiting us. He said he thought that a group of men from Operation Centurion, a task force attached to the mission, might be able to help us with the construction work. Sure enough, not many weeks later, Pete Nye arrived in Moldova and soon afterwards recruited a group of men experienced in building work to help in the construction. Hard work in hot sunshine transformed Casa Alex into the most delightful dwelling for six people. There was even time to plant in the ground that first spring and it quickly became an Eden. Gazing out of the windows of the house and standing on its impressive arched balcony overlooking the garden, we imagined the sheer pleasure in their surroundings those who moved out of the institution would experience.

Our growing experience in dealing with government and local officials with regard to such a move, together with our increasing credibility as a bona fide organisation, hastened the approval processes substantially. By August 2011 the house was beautifully ready and all the necessary official permission was obtained to move six people out of the institution. At the last minute two of the women for whom we had obtained permission decided very definitely that they wanted to stay where they were. In human terms this was a tragedy of the first order. They had been brain-washed by workers at the institution into believing that they would be very much worse-off with us than they were at present. Later that autumn, when we visited them at the institution, they both had had their hair shorn because of infection and were outside in the freezing cold without any kind of headwear. But the other four people—three women and one man— readily agreed to take the massive step to move out. Domnul Grişa was the father of Larisa, one of the three women, and they moved out together. Both were blind and Larisa was used to caring for her father. None of them regretted the move—in fact the very reverse was true and they kept telling us that they thought they had arrived in heaven itself in comparison to where they had been.

It was October, a few weeks after the four had moved out of the institution. The weather had already turned very cold and the first snow had fallen, though had not yet settled. We were having breakfast with those newly living in Casa Alex. The kitchen was warm and cosy and the conversation was lively. Everyone was expressing their appreciation of the food and of Casa Alex. Then, as often happens, especially during the first months after leaving the institution, the subject of conversation turned to their life as it had been over past decades. The other Larisa, who had been converted before she came to us, began to recount a series of experiences which left all of us deeply affected. Memories

spilled out of years in which those living in the institution
were regularly abused. She described horrifying incidents of
cruelty. We began to understand more clearly why she was
sometimes so emotionally overwrought.

That afternoon we were visiting the institution and the
three women from Casa Alex decided that they would like
to come with us for a visit to see some of their friends
there. It was a particularly bleak afternoon as we arrived
after having negotiated the very muddy tracks that led
us there. Hardly anyone was to be seen outside as it was
so cold. We went, as usual, from room to room greeting
one after another. Everywhere seemed dark and miserable
and because everyone was inside the stench was appalling.
Liliana and I made our way to one of the rooms where
someone we knew had been very ill on our previous visit.
This was a Jewish gentleman named Valentin and he had
infected bed sores and had been in great pain when we last
saw him. A member of our summer team had treated his
deep wound and another had prayed for him and sung to
him. His blanket had been covered in flies when we last saw
him. His bed was no longer there. We discovered that he had
died the previous Sunday and from all accounts in abject
neglect and in agony. Others in the room recounted the
details to us.

In one of the rooms we chatted to Slavic who was in his
thirties and without sight. He and a woman in the same
room told us of their experiences during time of *perestroika*
and before when the needs of those living in institutions
were all but forgotten when the rest of the country was
desperately trying to survive an upheaval of catastrophic
proportions. Slavic described how hundreds of children had

died, some of them poisoned by bad food, and buried in a hole without any kind of coffin or ceremony. Those with whom we were talking had lived through so very much. How our hearts went out to them!

One of the rooms was full of a suffocating stench and a number of women sitting listlessly on benches. We sang to them and longed that they should know the Saviour for themselves. That afternoon I was struck profoundly by the urgency of the need to take the Gospel and the love of Christ to such people. There was a wickedness about the whole situation that was deeply distressing. Staff accused us of taking people out of the institution to incarcerate them in prison in Sofia with complete loss of freedom. Their language was often foul and their treatment of those they were supposed to be caring for truly appalling. They often made them figures of ridicule and would laugh at their plight and sadness. I remember the hymn which says:

With none to hear their sighing for life and love and light
Unnumbered souls are dying and passing into night.

Liliana said to me that she felt as though sometimes we were working on the very edges of hell itself. We felt that to be true. Our only and powerful recourse was to our mighty Saviour who has spoiled principalities and powers and made an open show of them, triumphing over them in His Cross. We were in the hands of One who had bruised Satan under His foot and whose Name is higher than any other name. The spiritual battle in which we many times found ourselves was intense and often unremitting. We remembered that

"The name of the Lord is a strong tower; the righteous run to it and are safe" (Proverbs 18:10).

After that visit the three women whom we had brought from Casa Alex decided that they never wanted to visit the institution again. They were full of thankfulness to God who had delivered them from such a place and they laughed at those who said they had arrived in a prison. A few months later two more women, Mariana and Maria moved into Casa Alex from the same institution, bringing the number up to six.

A Story Still to be Told

... there remains very much land yet to be possessed
(Joshua 13:1)

There is a chorus which I learned as a young Christian which contains these words:

> *Follow, follow I would follow Jesus*
> *Anywhere, everywhere I would follow on*
> *Follow, follow I would follow Jesus*
> *Anywhere He leads me I would follow on*

Recently I have asked myself if I had known, when I sang those words so easily in my young days, where that following would take me, would I have sung those words so gladly? If

I had known that following would lead to meeting those in closed institutions, whose lives were marked by incalculable suffering, and if I had known the spiritual battles and challenges that lay ahead, would I still have followed? And my heart quietly answered yes.

"Swords drawn, swords drawn up to the gate of heaven" is a verse from another of Amy Carmichael's poems. Our warfare with the great enemy of our souls and with our own indwelling sin will not cease until we enter into His presence through the blood of the Lamb. The battle is often furious and unrelenting in the work to which God has called us, but we press on looking unto Jesus and trusting confidently in His final victory. And we wait for that rest that remains to the people of God and hail the day when the accuser of the brethren will be finally cast down and we will awake in glory never ever to sin again.

From the start of our involvement we have shared a conviction that this was a work which God Himself initiated and has sustained to the present day. It was not something brought about by the whim of man. Too many seemingly impossible obstacles would have made a man-made effort void from the beginning. Often the work has had a momentum which is not of us and we have known that to be the case. Often we have felt ourselves, as it were, running to keep up with the activity of God. Our own great frailty and lack of wisdom, strength, and sometimes of health, completely precluded the possibility of human resources winning the day. Here was a work which began and ended in God. And so we worship Him who seeks out and saves those who are sitting in darkness and in the shadow of death. We worship the One whose power alone called the work into being and whose great faithfulness has meant that we have never ever lacked for our needs. We take off our shoes in the presence of the Holy One of Israel who alone does wonders and we bow down before Him in awe.

Anea, Liliana and I will each have our "little day" and the work will need to be handed on to a new generation of labourers. We have no doubt but that the Lord Himself will raise up labourers to this most wonderful harvest field. Already we are beginning to see this happening and we rejoice. But I am thankful beyond words that that I was allowed to see a little of the beginnings of a work of God. To see such things was never, ever due to any merit on my part, but was all of His exceedingly great grace—this God who justifies the ungodly and makes the children of wrath into the children of the living God.

The first two years of Casa Alex proved to be anything but tranquil! We had underestimated the size of the challenge we were to face and the complex difficulties and sometimes problematic relationships with which we were confronted. Staff were often weary with the demands of supporting the six people who lived there. It continues to be a cause of great wonder to me to have seen that little by little, and in very different ways, the Lord began to woo each of those six individuals to the Saviour. We witnessed a powerful intervention of grace in lives that had been all but destroyed by sin and we marvelled as the Lord began to radically change lives and attitudes.

In June 2013, by the grace of God, a plot of land was purchased for the fourth house in a village called Căpriana. It is our intention that this should eventually be home to six women from the institution in the south. At the time of writing, in early 2014, the foundations have been dug for the house and the well has been drilled. How the Lord will meet the needs for the fourth house to be built and how He will once again overcome every obstacle that stands in the way of those six women moving into their new home is a story that has yet to be told. But do it He will, of that there is no doubt.

Căpriana is a most beautiful village surrounded by wooded hills. It is home to an ancient monastery so the village attracts many visitors. The site of the new house is a large plot of land which is peaceful in the extreme. Fruit and nut trees surround the land and goldfinches often perch on the top of the trees. The local church is but a few minutes walk down the hill and the pastor and his wife are eagerly awaiting our arrival there. What but the hand of God could have planned such goodness for His chosen ones? Yet again we silently marvel at His loving purposes.

In days of spiritual dearth in the UK there is encouragement to be found in discovering something of His work in other lands. Examples in these days abound of which this is just one. It is a quiet, largely unseen work, but it is a mighty work of His right hand and it is to Him alone that all glory is due!

> *Our God! our God! Thou shinest here;*
> *Thine own this latter day:*
> *To us Thy radiant steps appear;*
> *We watch Thy glorious way.*
>
> *Not only olden ages felt*
> *The presence of the Lord;*

Not only with the fathers dwelt
Thy Spirit and Thy Word.

Doth not the Spirit still descend
And bring the heavenly fire?
Doth not he still Thy church extend,
And waiting souls inspire?

Come, Holy Ghost, in us arise;
Be this Thy mighty hour,
And make Thy willing people wise
To know Thy day of power.